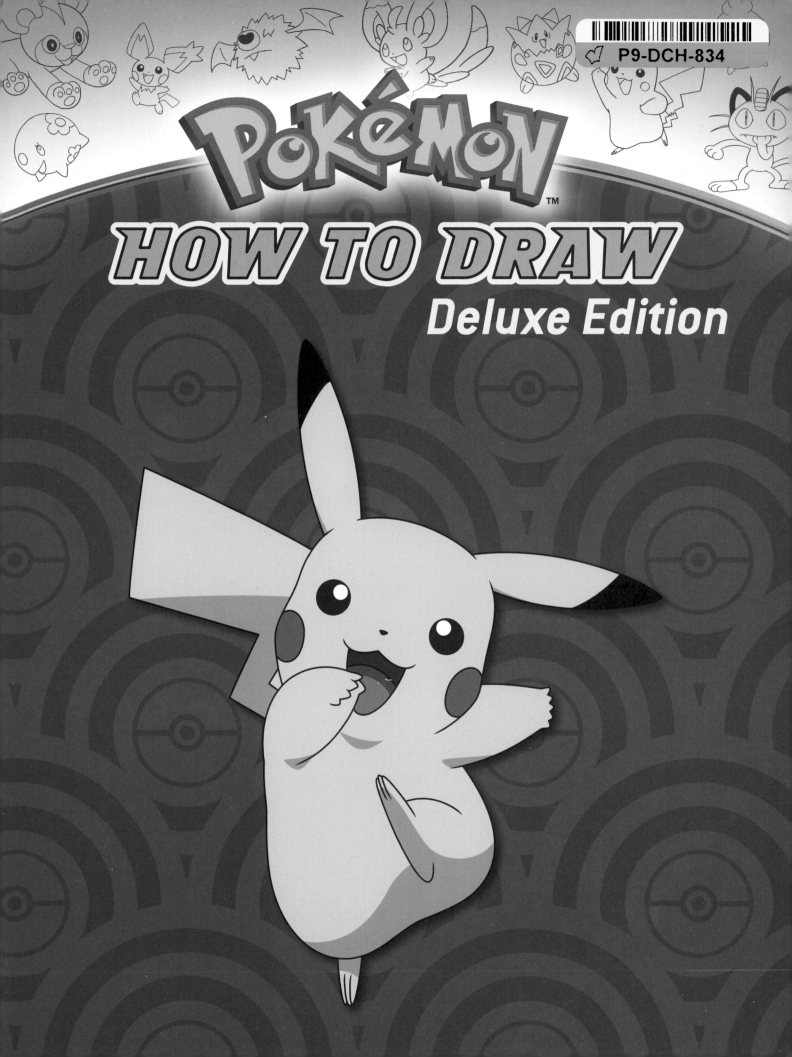

POKéMON

HOW TO DRAW

Deluxe Edition

ISBN 978-1-338-28381-5

10 9 8 7 6 5 4 3 2 1   18 19 20 21 22

Printed in Malaysia   106
First printing 2018

POKÉMON™
HOW TO DRAW
Deluxe Edition

Written by Maria S. Barbo, Tracey West, and Ron Zalme
Illustrations by Ron Zalme

SCHOLASTIC INC.

CONTENTS

INTRODUCTION

Are you ready to become a Pokémon drawing champ?
Get in gear! You will need:

- **Pencil**—Any basic graphite pencil should do the trick.
- **Paper**—Photocopy paper or tracing paper is terrific for sketching.
- **Eraser**—Try a soft one that won't smudge and has edges to get into tight spots.
- **Rulers, circle guides, ellipse (oval) guides, and shaped curves**—These help create a smooth, finished look for your drawing.
- **Color**—Try pens, markers, colored pencils, watercolors, paints, etc.

You may also want:
- A thin black marker
- Colored pencils
- Crayons
- Markers
- Watercolors and brushes
- Scrap paper

Getting Started:
WARM UP!

Step 1: Get loose! Shake out your arms.

Step 2: Stay loose! Practice drawing circles, squares, triangles, jellybeans, teardrops, squiggles, curvy lines, wavy lines, straight lines, and zigzags.

Step 3: Don't stress! Learning to draw takes time, practice, and lots of patience.

Tracing isn't cheating! It's a great way to practice drawing all the lines and shapes that make up a Pokémon.

Keep all your early drawings. It's fun to see how much better you get over time!

TOP FIVE
TRAINING TIPS

1. Back to basics. Start each drawing with the biggest, most basic steps. Save the details for the end.

2. Lighten up. Keep your lines light at first. They'll be easier to erase or draw over.

3. Break it down. Practice the hardest parts of each drawing on scrap paper before adding them to your masterpiece.

4. Work smudge-free. Keep a piece of scrap paper under your drawing hand so you don't smudge your picture.

5. Dark over light. Color in the lightest parts of each Pokémon first. If you use markers or paint, wait until the light colors are 100% dry before you add the dark parts. That way, your colors won't run into each other.

Spheres, cones, cubes, cylinders, and pyramids are the three-dimensional shapes that an artist must *think* in while drawing! Thinking in 3-D helps create the illusion of depth and volume in your artwork.

PIKACHU

Pika power! Pikachu are known for their sparkling personalities—and electrifying moves like Thunderbolt. But do you know what makes these amazing moves possible? Pikachu store up electric charges in their bodies, and they must release it from time to time to stay healthy. Have you stored up enough energy to draw this shocking Electric-type?

1

Start by drawing two lines that crisscross. Next draw a circle for the head. See how the bottom of the circle just touches the horizontal line in the cross? Now attach a squared-off U shape for the body and ovals for the hands and feet.

Draw the ears and arms. Where do you want to put the eyes and mouth? Use the crisscross guidelines to help you figure it out. Now take a minute to tweak the shape of Pikachu's face and body. Use the basic shapes you drew in Step One to guide you.

2

You're in the home stretch! Erase any lines you don't need. Now take a good look at your drawing. Pay special attention to the outline of the body. Do you need to make any changes?

4

3

Use zigzagging lines to add fingers. Zigzags also add detail to the tail. Then use short quick lines to make toes. Don't forget to draw in Pikachu's nose and the circles for super-charged cheeks.

POKÉMON TIP:

Smudge-proof your Pikachu! Color in the bright yellow body first. If you're using a marker, make sure it's completely dry before placing the darker colors on top of the yellow.

PIKACHU

Ash's Pikachu has been his constant companion ever since the Trainer started his Pokémon journey. Pikachu is awfully cute, but as everyone knows, you don't want to mess with its Electric-type attacks!

Where would Pikachu be without its lightning-bolt-shaped tail? Use straight lines to draw the tail peeking out from behind its body. Give Pikachu five tiny fingers on each hand and three toes on each foot. The lines on Pikachu's ears show where the yellow ends and the black tips begin.

2

From top to bottom, Pikachu's head is about the same size as its body. Remember that, and you'll have a top-notch Pikachu.

1

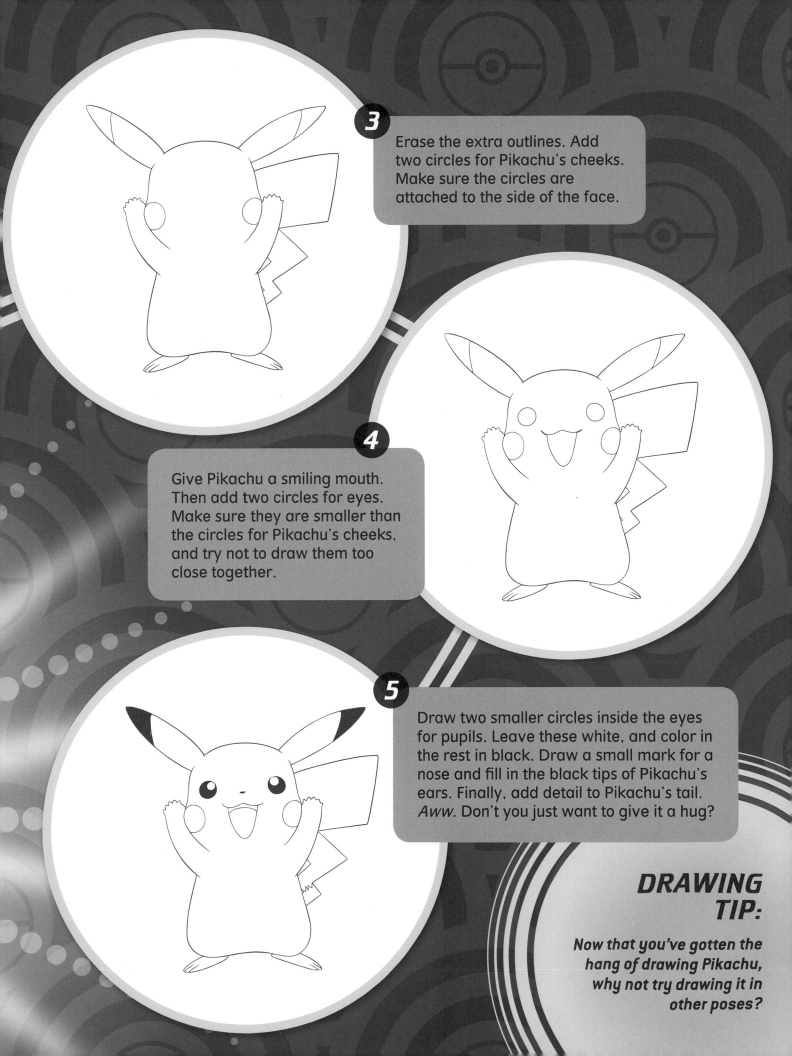

3 Erase the extra outlines. Add two circles for Pikachu's cheeks. Make sure the circles are attached to the side of the face.

4 Give Pikachu a smiling mouth. Then add two circles for eyes. Make sure they are smaller than the circles for Pikachu's cheeks, and try not to draw them too close together.

5 Draw two smaller circles inside the eyes for pupils. Leave these white, and color in the rest in black. Draw a small mark for a nose and fill in the black tips of Pikachu's ears. Finally, add detail to Pikachu's tail. *Aww.* Don't you just want to give it a hug?

DRAWING TIP:

Now that you've gotten the hang of drawing Pikachu, why not try drawing it in other poses?

BULBASAUR

Bulbasaur uses the big seed bulb on its back to soak up nutrients from the sun. This Grass-and-Poison-type has powerful moves like Razor Leaf and Vine Whip. Are you ready to show off your mighty drawing moves? Then let's take on Bulbasaur!

1 Start by breaking this drawing down into the simplest shapes. For Bulbasaur, that's a big, boxy head and half an oval for the body.

2 Draw a squished-heart shape for the mouth. Then add loose triangles for the eyes. Now sketch in the seed on Bulbasaur's back and three chubby legs. The lines for the legs closest to you go up and over the body. The lines for the leg farthest away from you are hidden behind the body.

Erase the guidelines you drew in Step One, and make any final corrections. Now that you know how to draw Bulbasaur, try drawing it in action. Add vines popping out of the seed on its back for Vine Whip!

4

3

Add details like spots on the skin and tiny triangles for the teeth and toenails. Inside each eye, draw a curved line next to an oval. Then add curves to the bulb on Bulbasaur's back.

CHARMANDER

Get out your reds, oranges, and yellows! The glowing flame on the tip of this Fire-type's tail shows that Charmander is in great shape. Are you in great shape for drawing? Warm up by scribbling basic shapes and lines on scrap paper.

1

Use this step to set up the entire drawing. How big is the head compared to the body? Where does the tail connect to the body? Don't worry about how your drawing looks at this stage. Just get down the basics.

Take a good look at Charmander's face. The eyes are set as wide as this Fire-type's smile. Now draw the outline of a flame on the tip of Charmander's tail.

2

Erase extra lines and smudges. Now stand back and compare your drawing to the one in the book. Is anything missing? Does one leg look like it's in front of the body while the other is behind it? If not, make sure you erased the right lines.

4

3 Take a minute to reshape the outline of Charmander's body. If you get confused, look at the final drawing to guide you. Then add details like teeth, eyes, claws, and more flames. Don't forget to add the curve of Charmander's belly!

SQUIRTLE

Squirtle's shell provides protection during battle, but this little Pokémon also fights back with winning Water-type moves like Aqua Tail and Water Gun. Once you learn how to draw Squirtle, you can use your winning moves to take on its more evolved forms: Wartortle, Blastoise, and Mega Blastoise.

2

Squirtle's right leg sticks straight out, but the left leg is bent. Position the arms at an angle next to Squirtle's head. If you squint your eyes, the whole body should look like the letter X.

1

The guidelines in this drawing are slanted. That's because Squirtle is leaning to the side, ready for action. Use the angled guidelines to sketch in the basic shapes of Squirtle's body and a curlicue for the tail.

4 Almost done! Erase any lines that are getting in the way. Does Squirtle look like it's ready to unleash a Rain Dance? Try drawing a burst of water blasting out of Squirtle's mouth, or some match-winning bubbles!

3 Detail time! Finish off the tail and shell with curved lines. Then draw two curved lines inside the mouth for the tongue and use zigzags for the fingers and toes. Study the different shapes inside the eyes before you draw them. For the pattern on Squirtle's tummy, start with a star, and then erase the pointy tips.

MEOWTH

Uh-oh! Team Rocket's Meowth looks like he's scared of something. Maybe he just heard that Jessie and James are out of food again. Knowing Meowth, he will do whatever it takes to get something yummy in his tummy.

Now give Meowth a tail. Notice how the tail starts where Meowth's body and legs meet. Round out the shape of Meowth's hands and feet. Then draw whiskers on the sides and top of his head—six whiskers in all.

Start with a sideways oval for Meowth's head. Add a body, arms, legs, hands, and feet. Meowth's ears are shaped like rounded triangles. Don't forget the jewel in the center of his head. It is shaped like a rectangle with rounded corners.

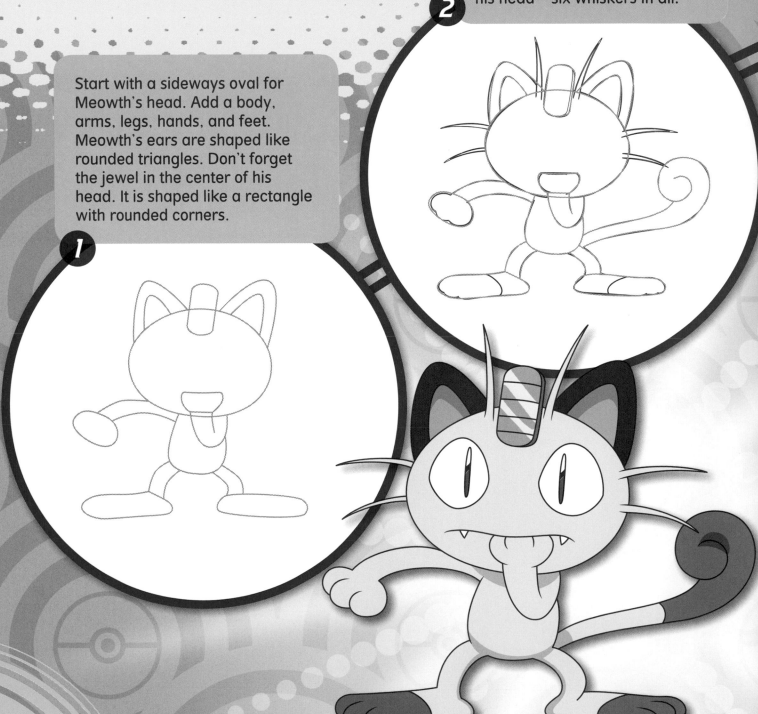

3
Give Meowth some toes and fingers on his paws and erase any extra lines. Add detail to the jewel and tail. Finally, give Meowth a wavy line for a mouth. Make sure it is curved down to give it a worried look.

4
Draw two pointy triangle teeth, then sketch in the eyes. As you can see, they are not perfect circles, but more like rounded diamonds.

5
Finish up Meowth by adding details to his eyes. Color in the black part on its ears. You've drawn Meowth—that's right!

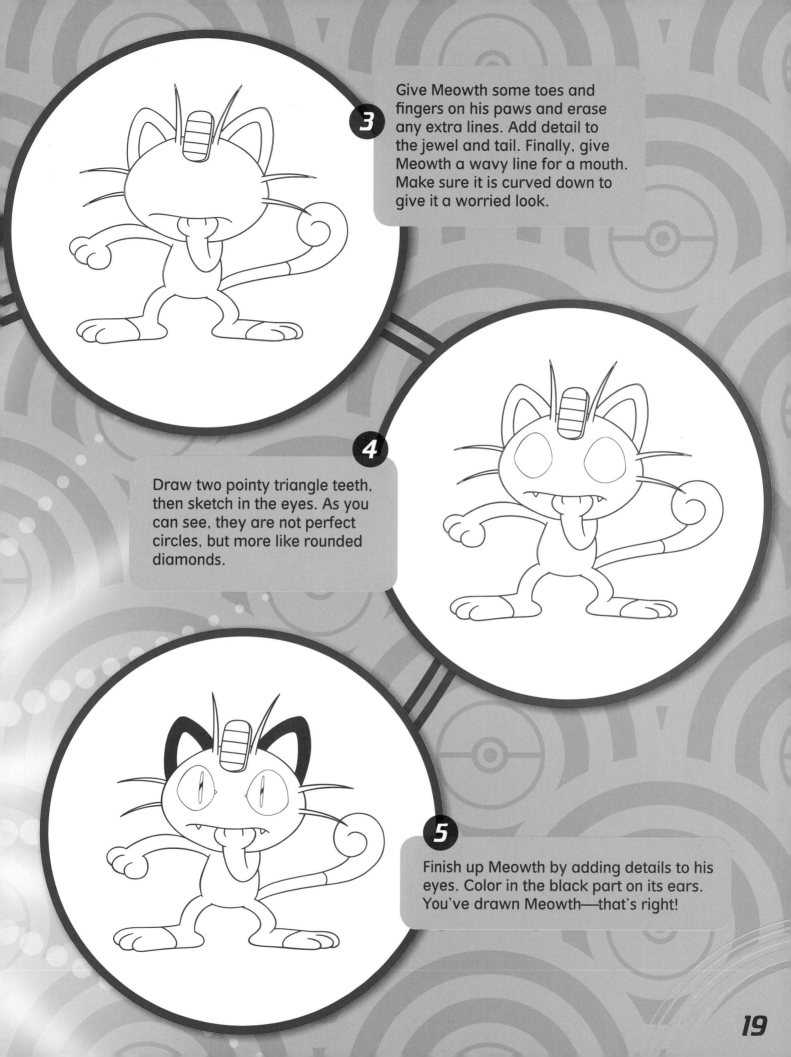

IGGLYBUFF

It's easy to see why Igglybuff is called the Balloon Pokémon. Besides being round, Igglybuff's body is very flexible and bouncy.

1

Start with a simple circle. Add two small circles for the eyes, then four curved lines for Igglybuff's tiny hands and feet.

Start adding detail to Igglybuff's eyes. Add its mouth next, and keep it smaller than the eyes. Don't forget to add the poofy shape to the top of Igglybuff's head.

2

3

No Igglybuff would be complete without the spiral-shaped curl above its eyes.

DRAWING TIP:

Now that you've drawn Igglybuff, see if you can draw its first evolved form, Jigglypuff! You'll start with the same simple circle.

CLEFFA

Cleffa's pointy ears and feet give its body a star shape. Some people say that because of its shape, Cleffa is the rebirth of a star.

1

Take away the pointy ears and feet, and Cleffa's body is shaped a lot like an egg. Start by drawing the egg shape, then add two rounded triangles at the top for ears.

Cleffa's eyes and cheeks are thin ovals. Add a wavy line for its mouth and two rounded triangles for hands and a curved line for the tail. Finally, add the feet and the cute curl on top of its head.

2

3

Fill in part of Cleffa's eyes with black, leaving some white on the top. When you're done, make sure you erase any lines you don't need.

DRAWING TIP:

To make a smiling mouth, draw a straight line and a curved line.

PICHU

Pichu, known as the Tiny Mouse Pokémon, is the pre-evolved form of Pikachu. These tiny Pokémon are not very good at controlling the electricity they store up. Occasionally they shock the people around them—and sometimes they even shock themselves!

Now that the head is in place, you can sketch in the two large ears! Use the crisscross guides to locate the eyes and mouth. Then move on to the arms.

First, draw the two arching action lines (shown in black). Using their placement as a guide, sketch the large circle for Pichu's head. The two crisscross guidelines on the head will give it a 3-D appearance and help you align the features. Next, draw the body shape and feet.

3 Most of the major construction is done, so you can start adding detail now. Pupils, cheeks, thumbs . . . and a tail, too! Add the M shapes to define the interior detail of each ear.

4 Darken the eyes, ears, tail, and bib; add a tongue; and you're almost done! As you finish, smooth out the angular construction lines to give a more natural feel to your character.

5 Cleanup time! Grab your eraser and carefully remove the sketched construction lines you used to build your drawing. Save only the linework that defines the character, then enhance those lines with darker pencil or pen.

CHIKORITA

In battle, Chikorita uses the leaf on top of its head to fight its opponent. The leaf may smell sweet, but look out! Its attacks can be dangerous.

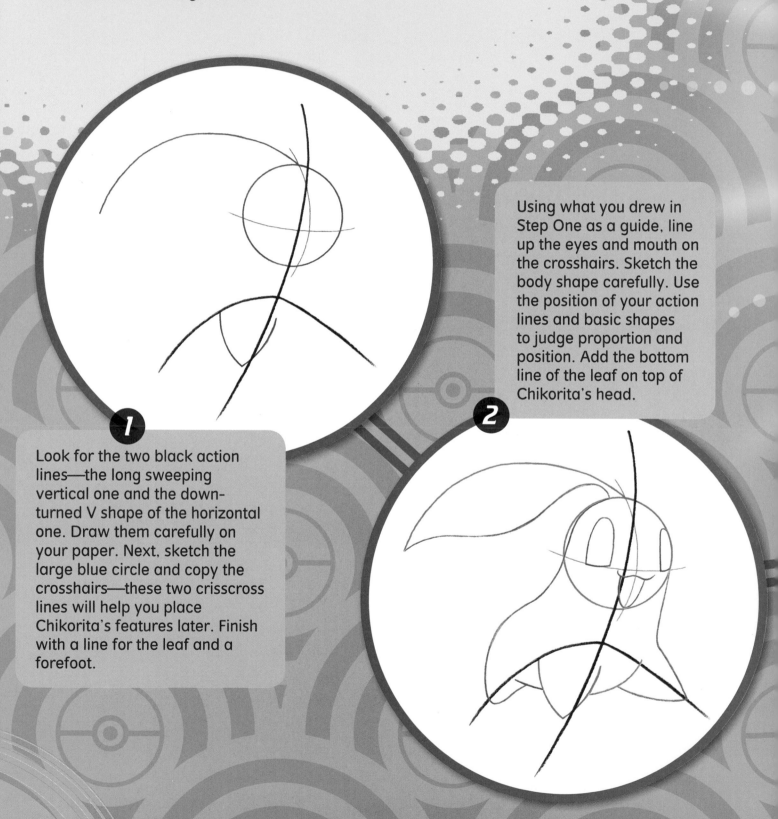

1

Look for the two black action lines—the long sweeping vertical one and the down-turned V shape of the horizontal one. Draw them carefully on your paper. Next, sketch the large blue circle and copy the crosshairs—these two crisscross lines will help you place Chikorita's features later. Finish with a line for the leaf and a forefoot.

2

Using what you drew in Step One as a guide, line up the eyes and mouth on the crosshairs. Sketch the body shape carefully. Use the position of your action lines and basic shapes to judge proportion and position. Add the bottom line of the leaf on top of Chikorita's head.

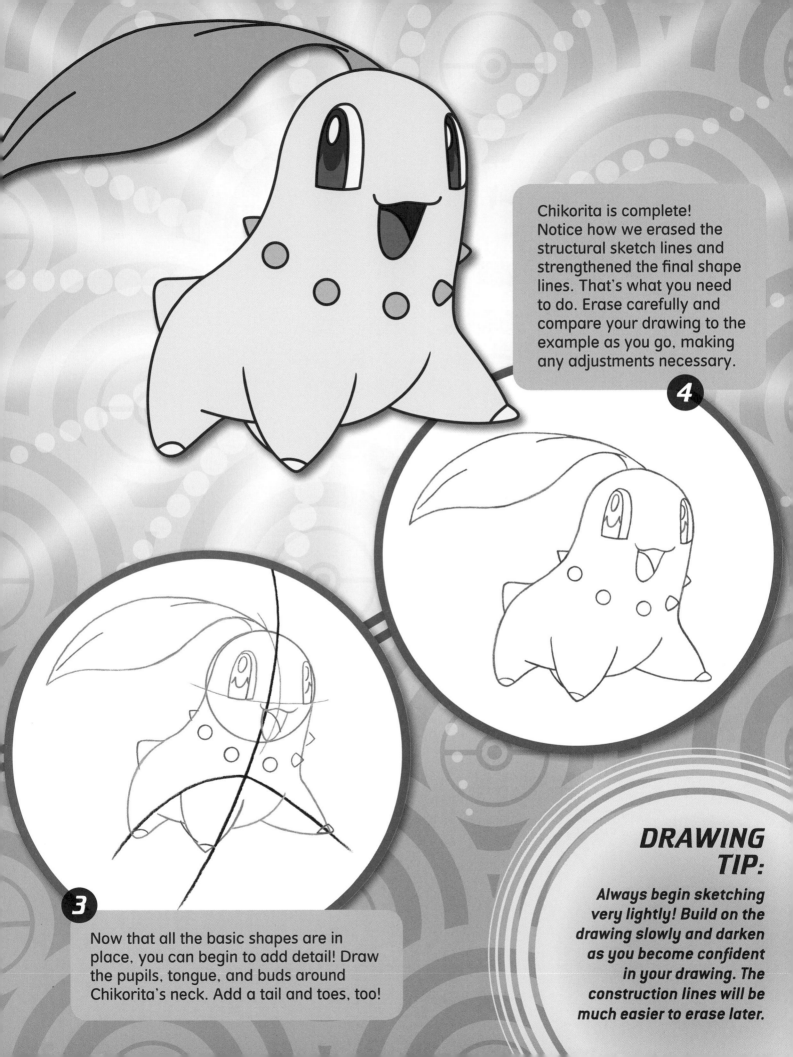

Chikorita is complete! Notice how we erased the structural sketch lines and strengthened the final shape lines. That's what you need to do. Erase carefully and compare your drawing to the example as you go, making any adjustments necessary.

4

3

Now that all the basic shapes are in place, you can begin to add detail! Draw the pupils, tongue, and buds around Chikorita's neck. Add a tail and toes, too!

DRAWING TIP:

Always begin sketching very lightly! Build on the drawing slowly and darken as you become confident in your drawing. The construction lines will be much easier to erase later.

CYNDAQUIL

The flames on Cyndaquil's back can tell you a lot about its mood. If the fire seems to sputter, this little Pokémon is probably tired. But if the flames are high and hot, look out—that means Cyndaquil is angry!

1

This time, the horizontal black action line sweeps upward. Copy both lines onto your paper. Next, sketch the head circle over the horizontal action line and the body circle below it. Note how the crosshairs establish the direction the face is pointing. Add a loose outline (on the right) to define a boundary for the flames . . . it doesn't need to be exact.

Add the nose and legs in position over your sketch. Next, place the mouth and eye, then put some flame detail along the back.

2

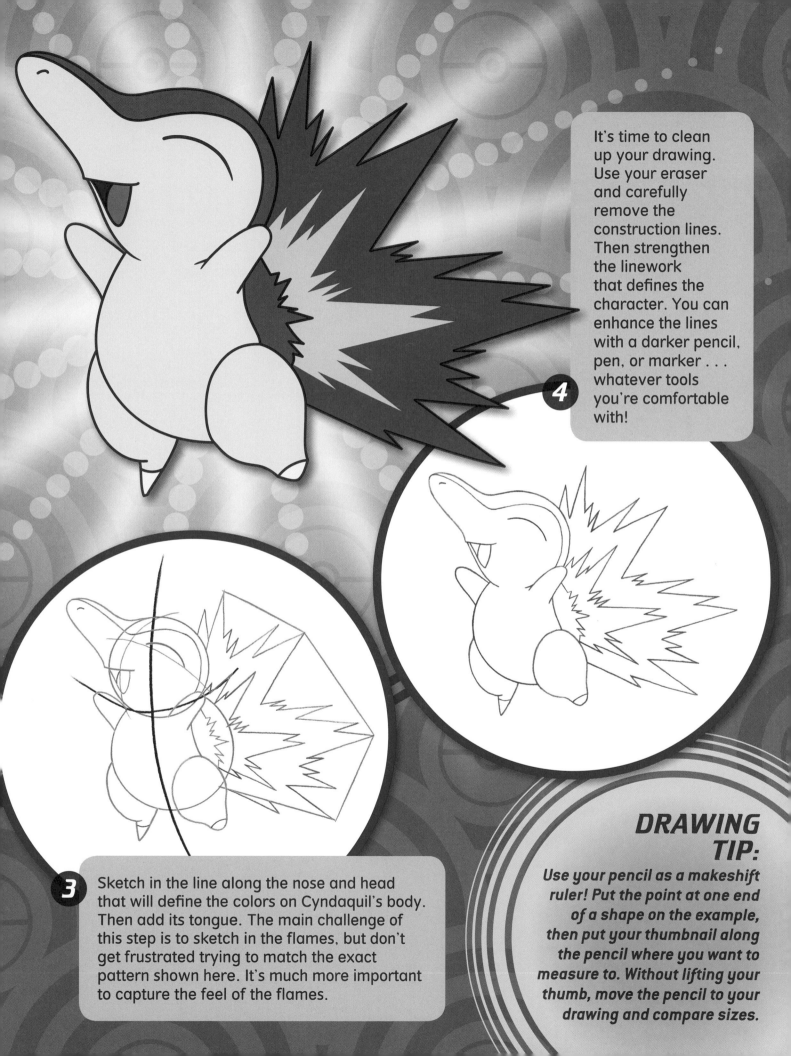

It's time to clean up your drawing. Use your eraser and carefully remove the construction lines. Then strengthen the linework that defines the character. You can enhance the lines with a darker pencil, pen, or marker . . . whatever tools you're comfortable with!

4

3 Sketch in the line along the nose and head that will define the colors on Cyndaquil's body. Then add its tongue. The main challenge of this step is to sketch in the flames, but don't get frustrated trying to match the exact pattern shown here. It's much more important to capture the feel of the flames.

DRAWING TIP:

Use your pencil as a makeshift ruler! Put the point at one end of a shape on the example, then put your thumbnail along the pencil where you want to measure to. Without lifting your thumb, move the pencil to your drawing and compare sizes.

TOTODILE

Totodile is often playful, but nonetheless, you should handle it with care. Sometimes it will nibble on friends affectionately, but its superstrong jaws have been known to injure Trainers by accident.

1

Draw the action lines lightly and place the large head circle, with its crosshairs, on the vertical one. Next, locate and sketch the large oval for the hip of the leg. This will make it much easier to copy the shapes for the rest of the body and tail.

2

Sketch the eye shapes and then carefully add the nose and mouth. Now sketch in the arms and feet. You can also begin to add tail-spikes, starting with the one closest to the end of the tail.

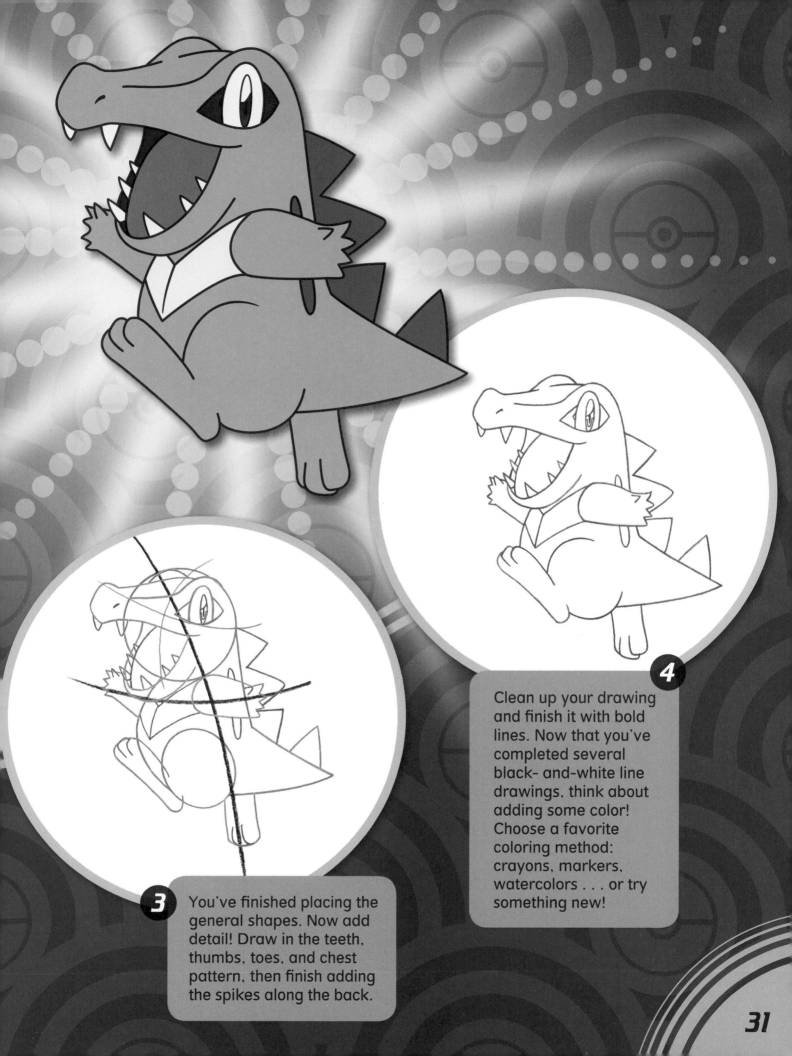

3 You've finished placing the general shapes. Now add detail! Draw in the teeth, thumbs, toes, and chest pattern, then finish adding the spikes along the back.

4 Clean up your drawing and finish it with bold lines. Now that you've completed several black- and-white line drawings, think about adding some color! Choose a favorite coloring method: crayons, markers, watercolors . . . or try something new!

TOGEPI

Togepi's shell is filled with happiness. It soaks up cheerful vibes from the people and Pokémon around it, and then it uses these warm fuzzies as energy.

1

After copying the simple set of crisscross action lines, draw the very large circle shape for the body. Sketch the two crosshairs and add the simple ovals for the feet.

Add three of the spikes on top of Togepi's head, then draw its face. The jagged lines of its shell don't need to be perfect as long as the right feel is there. Make sure they follow a curve around the shell, so your drawing will have some dimension to it.

2

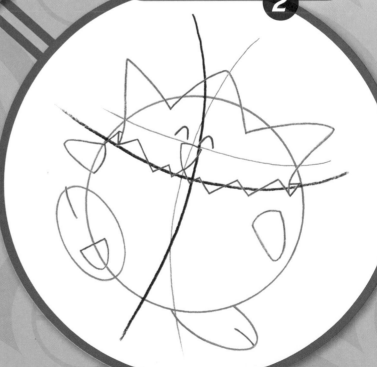

3

If you didn't add the arms and toes in the last step, add them now! Then sketch in two more spikes on top of the head. Finish this step by drawing the triangular design shapes on its shell.

4

Get rid of those construction lines and finish up in your favorite style! Remember, you're the artist, so decisions about how to create are yours to make. Imagination and experimentation are the best tools at your disposal, so use them!

MARILL

When Marill gets hungry, it dives underwater to look for plants to eat. But its tail floats on the surface and sometimes acts as an anchor by wrapping itself around a tree.

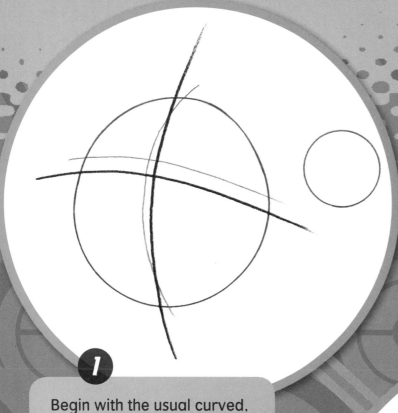

1

Begin with the usual curved, crossed action lines and place the very large oval over them. Notice that it's almost a circle, but just a bit pinched toward the top. Add the crosshairs for the features on Marill's face, then draw a smaller circle to the right of the big one.

Sketch the eyes, nose, and mouth along the crosshair axis, and then add the two large ovals for ears. Finish roughing in your character by adding the arms and feet.

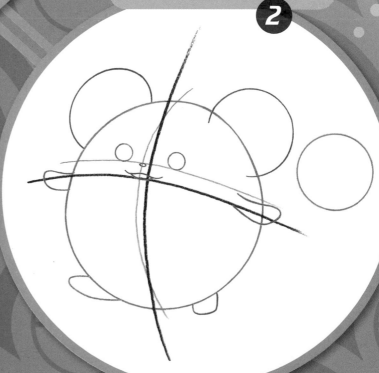

2

Clean up with your eraser, and focus on the shapes and details. Compare your drawing to the example. Have you missed anything? Make any corrections necessary and consider your color options!

4

3

The rest is detail! Draw the inner ear ovals, and then make a large circle on Marill's chest area to define its color design. Connect the smaller tail circle to the main body with two jagged lines. It's not important that they be drawn exactly as long as they get across the right idea.

DRAWING TIP:

It's not necessary to buy circle guides and other shapes. You can use various household items like buttons, coins, cups, and cans . . . anything round can work as a guide!

TEDDIURSA

Teddiursa loves honey! Its paws are often soaked in it, and it can change the honey's flavor by mixing in different kinds of pollen and berries.

1

Action lines, large head circle, crosshairs, body shape, and ears. No matter how complex the drawing, you break it down into a series of easier steps: foundation, basic shapes, and detail.

Draw the eyes, nose, and mouth in position over the guides, then sketch in the arms, feet, and tail. Last, but not least, put in some detail for the ears.

2

3

Add that crescent on Teddiursa's forehead! And don't forget the cheek lines, claws, tongue, and toes. Almost done!

4

Erase your unwanted sketch lines, and then strengthen the lines you want to keep. Now that you know the basics, try drawing Teddiursa in a pose of your own! The shapes will remain basically the same, but the positioning will change.

MUDKIP

Mudkip is a Pokémon that really knows how to get creative! Its fin is so sensitive to the air and water around it, it can swim with its eyes closed. What's your creative vision for this drawing? Will Mudkip take up the whole paper? Or will it splash off into the sunset?

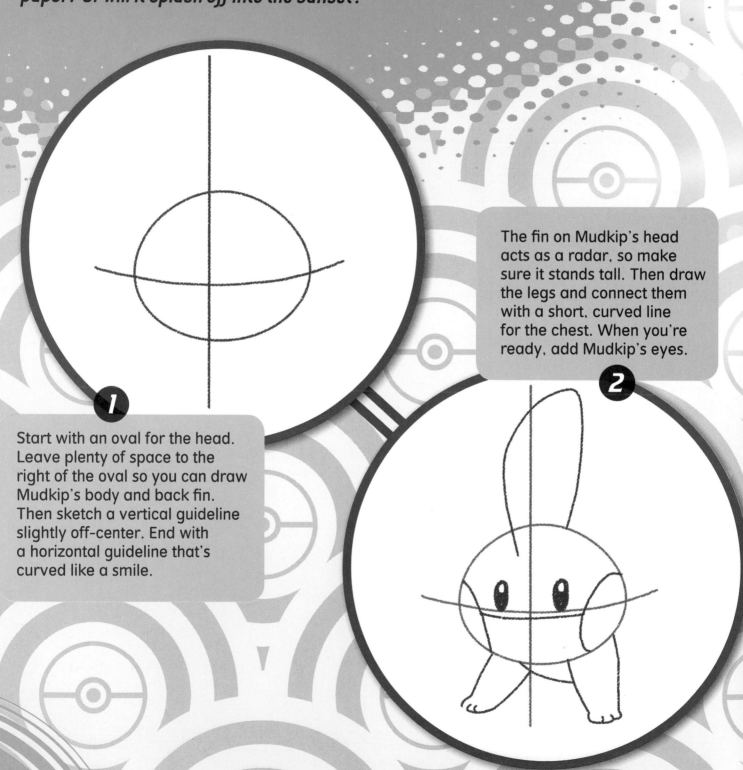

The fin on Mudkip's head acts as a radar, so make sure it stands tall. Then draw the legs and connect them with a short, curved line for the chest. When you're ready, add Mudkip's eyes.

1

Start with an oval for the head. Leave plenty of space to the right of the oval so you can draw Mudkip's body and back fin. Then sketch a vertical guideline slightly off-center. End with a horizontal guideline that's curved like a smile.

2

Color time! The bright orange on Mudkip's cheeks contrast the serene blues of its body. If you're using colored pencils, lightly shade the blue parts of the body first, and then press harder in the areas where you want to create shadows.

4

3 Trace over the lines in Mudkip's body on scrap paper a few times before adding them to your piece. Tracing is great practice! Then add two curved lines for the mouth to give this Water-type Pokémon a *swim*-sational smile!

DRAWING TIP:

The steps you've learned are not just for Pokémon . . . apply them to all your drawings. How would you be constructed step-by-step?

TREECKO

Treecko is always calm and ready to face any challenge! Does it need to scale a wall or take down a bigger opponent with Quick Attack? No sweat! Are you calm about this drawing? Trace the last step on tracing paper before you begin. It helps you get a sense of where all the shapes and lines will go. And it's a great way to practice!

1

Use this step to set up the whole drawing. How big is Treecko's head compared to the body? Which direction is Treecko facing? Where does the tail connect to the body? Don't worry about making it perfect. Just do the basics.

Now take a minute to get the angles right in the arms and legs. Does one leg look like it's stretched in front of the other? Is the back arm raised and ready to Pound? Great! Then add curved shapes for the eye and nose.

2

3

Draw a crescent moon at the base of Treecko's belly and slits to the eyes. Then sketch in the curved toes and fingers. Before you add the tail, practice drawing sweeping S curves on scrap paper. But watch out! Treecko uses its tail to Slam foes.

4

Cleanup time! Erase extra lines. Then compare your drawing to the one in the book. Is anything missing? Did you refine the shape of Treecko's head and add nostrils? Great! Now get out your markers and get ready to color!

TORCHIC

With moves like Flamethrower and Fire Spin, this sweet Chick Pokémon can breathe flames and fireballs! But don't sweat this sketch! There's a secret to creating motion in a Pokémon drawing. Start with a tilted guideline. Torchic's whole body will look like it's leaning to one side. Curve that same guideline, and Torchic will look like it's running right at you!

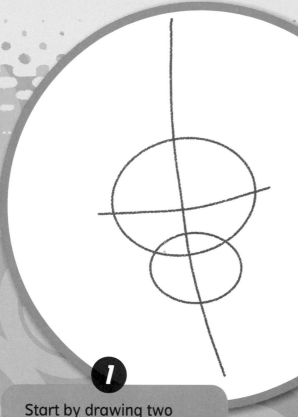

1

Start by drawing two slightly curved guidelines that criss-cross. Make sure they are slightly angled. Draw an oval for a head where the two lines meet. Then add a smaller oval for the body. The ovals should overlap.

Lay in the basic shapes for the face, wings, and feet. Keep your lines loose and light at this stage—you may need to erase them later. Practice sketching the foot on scrap paper a few times before adding it to your drawing.

2

3

It's all about the details! Draw a U-shaped line inside the mouth to give it depth. Want to make Torchic look like it's running? The back leg is behind the body and off the ground, so you only have to draw the toes!

4

Clean up your drawing. Then hold it up to a mirror. Spot anything that needs to be fixed? What lines or shapes would you change to make your drawing even better? Now, quick! Color in Torchic before it evolves into Combusken!

ARON

This Steel-and Rock-type Pokémon has big moves like Heavy Slam and Headbutt. Are you ready to show off your drawing moves? Here's a pro tip: If a drawing has too many details or looks too complicated, pick a place to start—like the body or head—and work on one section at a time. Breaking down a big job into a smaller one can totally make it easier to tackle!

2

Next focus on the head. Draw three circles along the vertical guideline— and a squiggly line along the right edge. Now look at the body. Draw a short line connecting the head and spine. Then add a rounded leg and a tail made of three short lines.

1

Start by sketching an oval that overlaps a smaller circle. Then draw a straight line down the middle of the oval. Add a curved line that runs from the back of the circle through the oval. Think of this guideline as Aron's spine.

4

Ready to rock this drawing with color? Aron's underbelly is a dark gray like steel, but its body armor is pale gray. Try lightly shading the shadows with a gray pencil while letting the white of the paper show through in the highlights.

3

More details! Add two more cone-shaped legs and two curved lines on the belly. Draw an oval on Aron's side. Then add details to the head, like the eye and the curve of the forehead. Are any details missing?

PLUSLE

This positive Pokémon can short out the electricity in its body and use shocking moves like Thunder Wave, Spark, and Electro Ball! Plusle and Minun definitely have a similar style—but the shape of their tails and the symbols on their cheeks are totally one of a kind!

1 Start with a circle and two guidelines. The guidelines in this drawing are slanted and curved to show that Plusle is taking a running leap.

2 Lightly sketch in the outlines of the body and ears. Plusle's right ear is bent to show movement. Then add a wide-open smile, two round cheeks, and Plusle's oval eyes.

3 Take a second to sketch a short curved line inside the mouth to give it dimension. Then draw the rest of the details, like the circles inside the ears. Did you notice that Plusle's tail and cheeks look like plus signs?

4 Erase any extra lines. Did you miss any details—like the bright red accents on Plusle's face and tail? Now that you can draw Plusle, draw it showering its teammates in happy red sparks!

MINUN

Now that you can draw Plusle, try your hand at its teammate, Minun. This Electric-type Pokémon uses pom-poms made of sparks for cheering on its teammates. Will Minun spark your imagination?

Use light lines to sketch the outline of Minun's body. Then draw two long ovals on top of the head. These ears are almost as long as the whole body. Feeling charged up? Start adding details to the face, like eyes and cheeks.

First sketch an oval. Then draw two curved guidelines. The curves show motion. Try drawing the guidelines super fast. Believe it or not, starting with quickly sketched guidelines can make your final drawing look more dynamic!

3

Minun's tail is a rectangle. Tilt it away from the body. Then draw an upside-down U shape for the leg facing *away* from the tail. Now add details to the face and ears. Does your Minun already look like it's skipping ahead?

4

Erase the guidelines and make any fixes. Color Minun's body with a yellow marker. Once that's dry, use baby blue for the ears, cheeks, hands, and tail. Now that you can draw both Plusle and Minun, draw them sparking up a new friendship—or working together to cheer on Ash and Pikachu!

LOTAD

Want the lowdown on Lotad? They float on the surface of ponds and lakes. It's a totally chill way to live! You can chill out before facing this drawing by practicing sketching its leaflike hat on scrap paper first. Feeling more confident? Get ready to dive in!

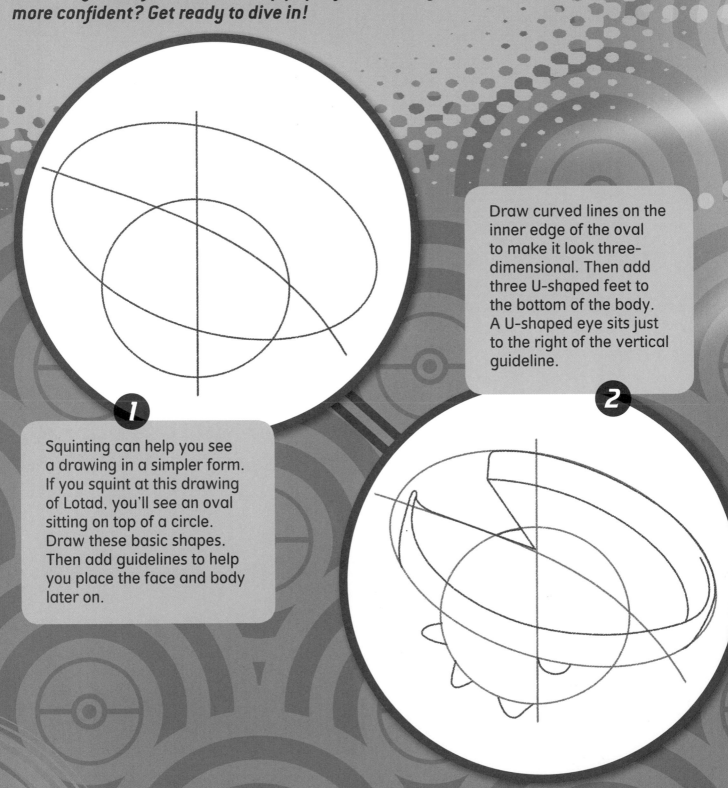

1

Squinting can help you see a drawing in a simpler form. If you squint at this drawing of Lotad, you'll see an oval sitting on top of a circle. Draw these basic shapes. Then add guidelines to help you place the face and body later on.

2

Draw curved lines on the inner edge of the oval to make it look three-dimensional. Then add three U-shaped feet to the bottom of the body. A U-shaped eye sits just to the right of the vertical guideline.

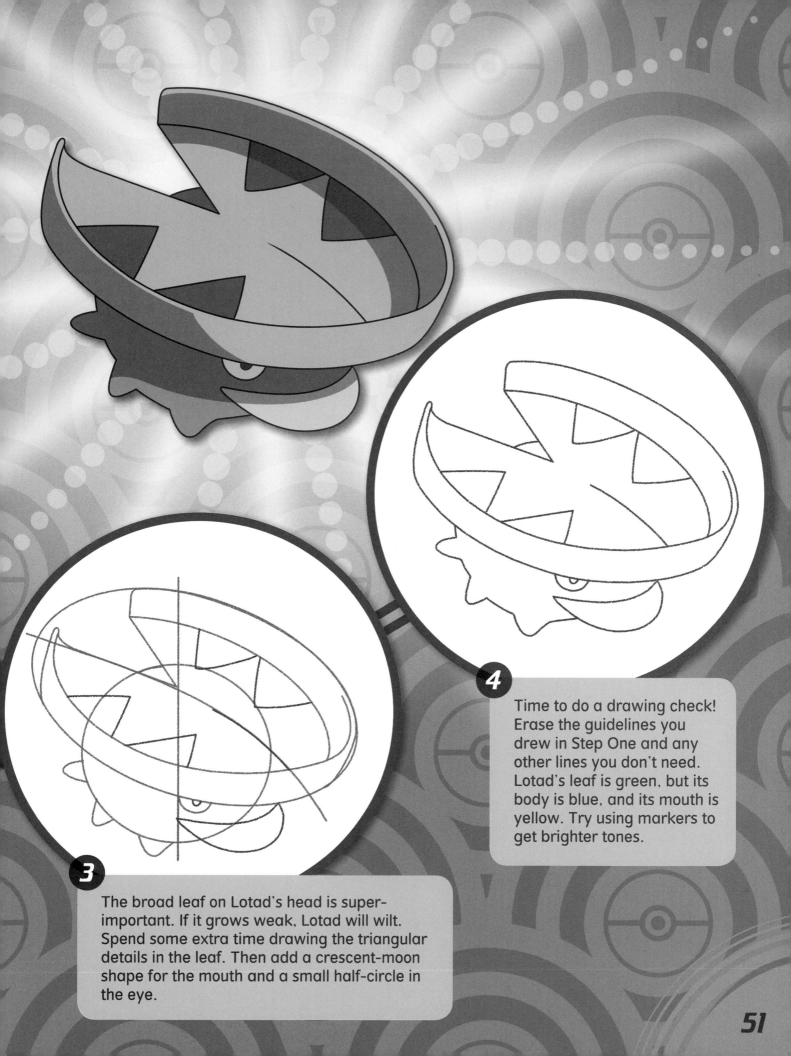

4

Time to do a drawing check! Erase the guidelines you drew in Step One and any other lines you don't need. Lotad's leaf is green, but its body is blue, and its mouth is yellow. Try using markers to get brighter tones.

3

The broad leaf on Lotad's head is super-important. If it grows weak, Lotad will wilt. Spend some extra time drawing the triangular details in the leaf. Then add a crescent-moon shape for the mouth and a small half-circle in the eye.

PIPLUP

Piplup may be cute, but it's also one tough—and proud—Pokémon! Lots of Trainers in the Sinnoh region choose to start their Pokémon journey with this Water-type. You can choose to start your drawing training with Piplup, but here's a tip: Don't be too proud to make mistakes. You're just starting out!

1

This drawing is all about ovals. Start with two crisscrossing guidelines. Then use them to place the ovals for the head, flippers, and feet. Now draw the guidelines on the face.

Look at the face. The middle of the nose sits right where the two guidelines meet. Now draw the body around the ovals you drew for the flippers and feet in Step One.

2

Erase the guidelines from Step One and any other lines you don't need. Congratulations! Is a cute little Piplup looking back at you?

4

3

Add details like Piplup's tail. Then draw curved lines on its feet for toes. Finally, darken in the eyes and add a zigzag pattern on its forehead.

DRAWING TIP:

Color in Piplup with cool shades of turquoise and aqua. You can use a white colored pencil for Piplup's eyes and the ovals on its chest. But if you are drawing on white paper, you can just leave those areas empty.

TURTWIG

This Grass-type Pokémon is the first partner Pokémon of choice for lots of Trainers in the Sinnoh region. It has powerful moves like Leaf Storm, and it loves living near water! Turtwig's shell is made of soil and uses photosynthesis to produce energy in battle. One thing is for sure: As an artist-in-training, you can learn a lot from Turtwig. It's brave and confident.

2

Begin drawing the face. Then add details to the shell on Turtwig's back. Don't forget to draw the back leg. And tweak the shape of the other legs. Now work on the leaves on top of Turtwig's head and attach them to a cone.

1

Start with an oval for the head. Then attach the shape for the body. Now draw ovals for the feet. Finally, draw a big U shape up at the top of your drawing. This will become leaves later on.

Time to clean up your drawing! Did you draw the jaw-plate? Take a minute to redraw any parts that need fixing.

4

3

Draw two lines that slant down at the top of the ovals you drew for eyes. Remember to leave an oval of white for the highlight in each eye. Now add details to the body and legs.

DRAWING TIP:

Color your creation! Shadows can help make a drawing look 3-D. They are usually warm in tone—made up of colors like reds, violets, and browns.

CHIMCHAR

Chimchar heats things up with moves like Flame Wheel and Fire Spin. Its rear end is always on fire—even in the rain! If you live in the Sinnoh region and want to start your Pokémon journey with a fiery friend, Chimchar is the Pokémon for you!

1 This Pokémon is dancing around, so start by drawing the guidelines on an angle. Then add the basic shapes for the arms, legs, hands, feet, and body.

2 Add the jaw and mouth to the bottom of the circle you drew for a head. Then place the eyes and attach basic shapes for the hair and ears. Now connect the shapes you drew in Step One to create the body.

Great job! Erase extra lines so you can see your drawing. Did you remember to draw the swirl on Chimchar's tummy? What about the bangs? They look like the letter M.

4

3

There are lots of details in this step so take your time. Use your training to draw Chimchar's eyes. Then add short, quick lines for the eyebrows, nose, and teeth. The tail is also really important. Keep the flame half-hidden behind Chimchar's body.

DRAWING TIP:

Use warm, fiery tones like burnt orange, yellow, and red to color your creation. Keep the color lighter in the highlights.

MANTYKE

This friendly Pokémon looks like a mini-version of its evolved form, Mantine. Mantyke usually live near Remoraid. The pattern on Mantyke's back can change depending on which region it lives in. Can you tell why it's known as the Kite Pokémon?

Start by drawing two guidelines that crisscross and curve. Keep them really light so you can erase them later on.

1

Draw a big oval on top of the lines. The two lines meet in the middle of the oval. Then use the horizontal guideline to help you position the fins.

2

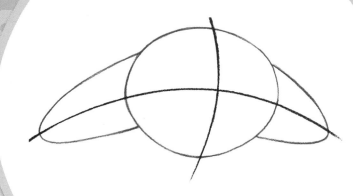

3 Use the lines from Step One as a guide to place the eyes and mouth. Then draw two antenna feelers at the top of Mantyke's oval body.

4 It's time to add details! Draw the curving line that runs around Mantyke's body. Then add another line for the tongue. Finally, darken the details on Mantyke's bright happy eyes.

5 Erase the guidelines from Step One and any other lines you don't need. Now take a minute to fine-tune the outline of the body.

DRAWING TIP:

Chase away the blues . . . with color! Shade Mantyke with two different shades of blue. Then go back and trace over the lines with a thin black marker.

AIPOM

It only takes one look at Aipom's smiling face to know this Normal-type Pokémon isn't aggressive. But it is energetic! It lives in treetops and can leap from tree to tree all day with the help of its nimble tail. It relies so much on its tail that its hands have lost some of their dexterity.

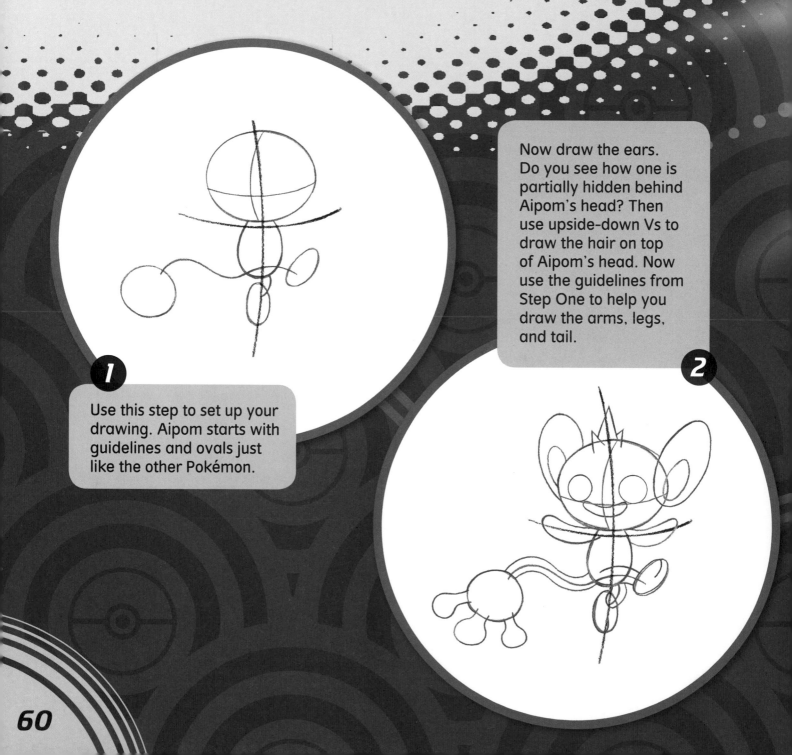

1

Use this step to set up your drawing. Aipom starts with guidelines and ovals just like the other Pokémon.

2

Now draw the ears. Do you see how one is partially hidden behind Aipom's head? Then use upside-down Vs to draw the hair on top of Aipom's head. Now use the guidelines from Step One to help you draw the arms, legs, and tail.

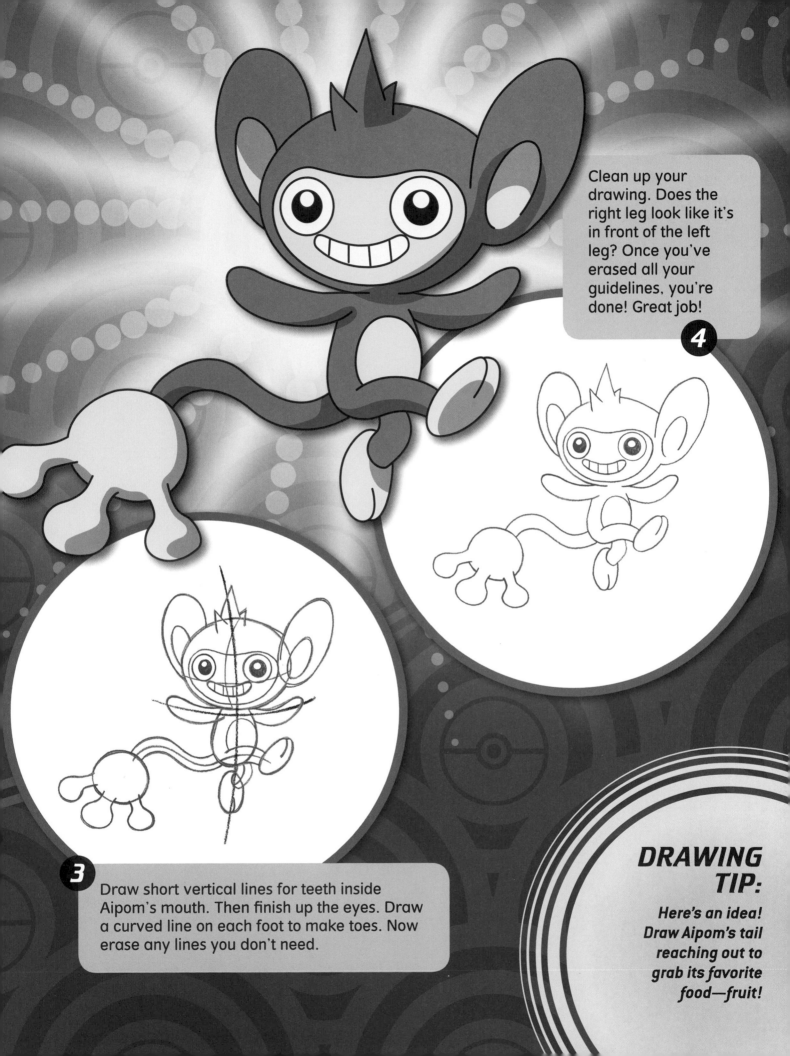

Clean up your drawing. Does the right leg look like it's in front of the left leg? Once you've erased all your guidelines, you're done! Great job!

4

3

Draw short vertical lines for teeth inside Aipom's mouth. Then finish up the eyes. Draw a curved line on each foot to make toes. Now erase any lines you don't need.

DRAWING TIP:

Here's an idea! Draw Aipom's tail reaching out to grab its favorite food—fruit!

BUIZEL

Dive in! This Water-type Pokémon has splash-tastic moves like Whirlpool and Sonic Boom, and it evolves into Floatzel. Drawing Buizel may look tough, but you've been training hard. Take a cue from this playful Pokémon and have fun while you draw. You're not battling for a Gym badge!

1 Get your guidelines ready. Then draw ovals for the head, arms, and feet. Now connect the feet with a curved line.

Take it slow and break it down. You're a pro! Connect the shapes you drew in Step One to draw the body. Then add a big Y-shaped tail. Can you use the guidelines to help you place the eye?

2

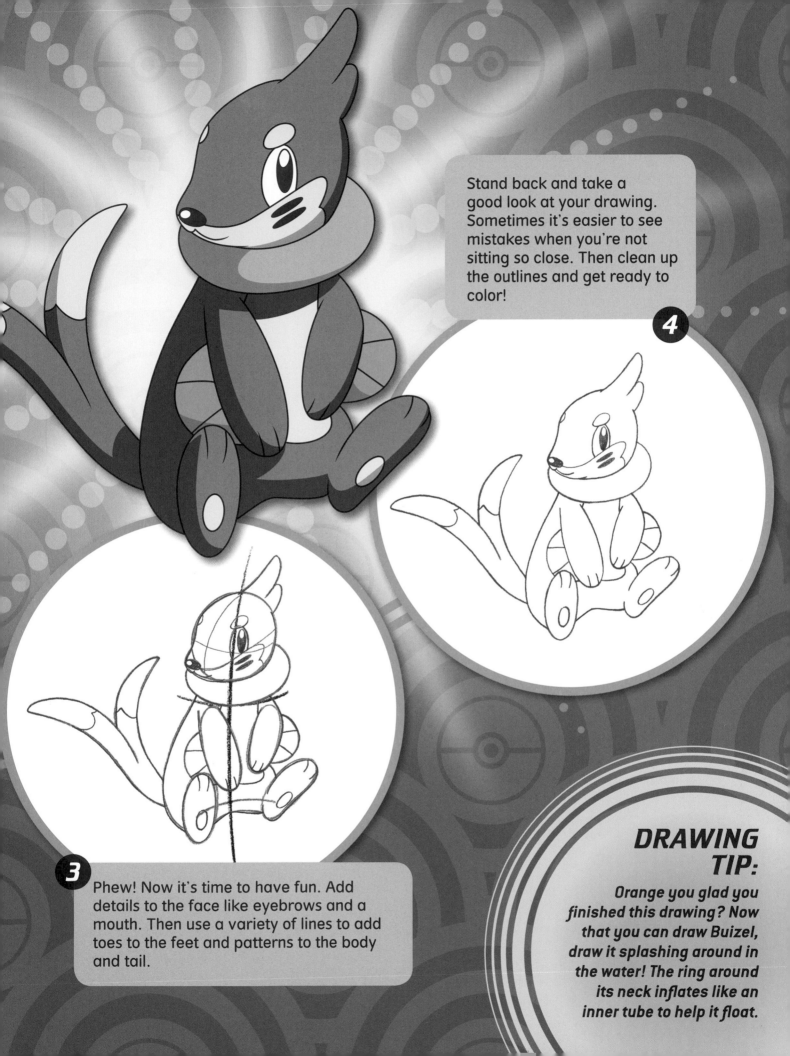

Stand back and take a good look at your drawing. Sometimes it's easier to see mistakes when you're not sitting so close. Then clean up the outlines and get ready to color!

4

3

Phew! Now it's time to have fun. Add details to the face like eyebrows and a mouth. Then use a variety of lines to add toes to the feet and patterns to the body and tail.

DRAWING TIP:

Orange you glad you finished this drawing? Now that you can draw Buizel, draw it splashing around in the water! The ring around its neck inflates like an inner tube to help it float.

LICKILICKY

As its name suggests, this pink, plump Pokémon has a super-long tongue. Lickilicky can use this tongue to grab objects or even use it to battle opponents—look out for its Lick attack! This Lickilicky looks pretty friendly, but if you try to befriend it, you might want to bring a towel along. Get too close to a Lickilicky and you could end up covered in its drool!

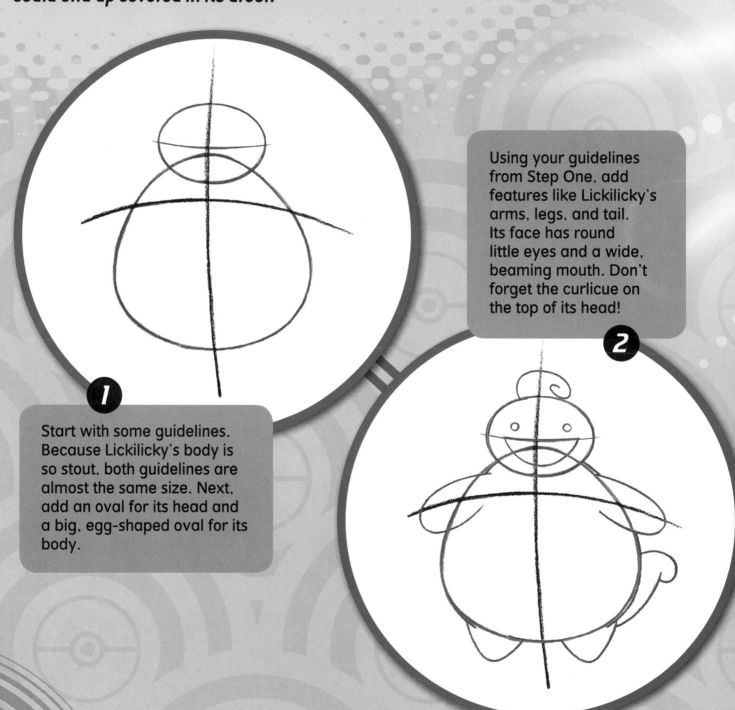

Using your guidelines from Step One, add features like Lickilicky's arms, legs, and tail. Its face has round little eyes and a wide, beaming mouth. Don't forget the curlicue on the top of its head!

2

1

Start with some guidelines. Because Lickilicky's body is so stout, both guidelines are almost the same size. Next, add an oval for its head and a big, egg-shaped oval for its body.

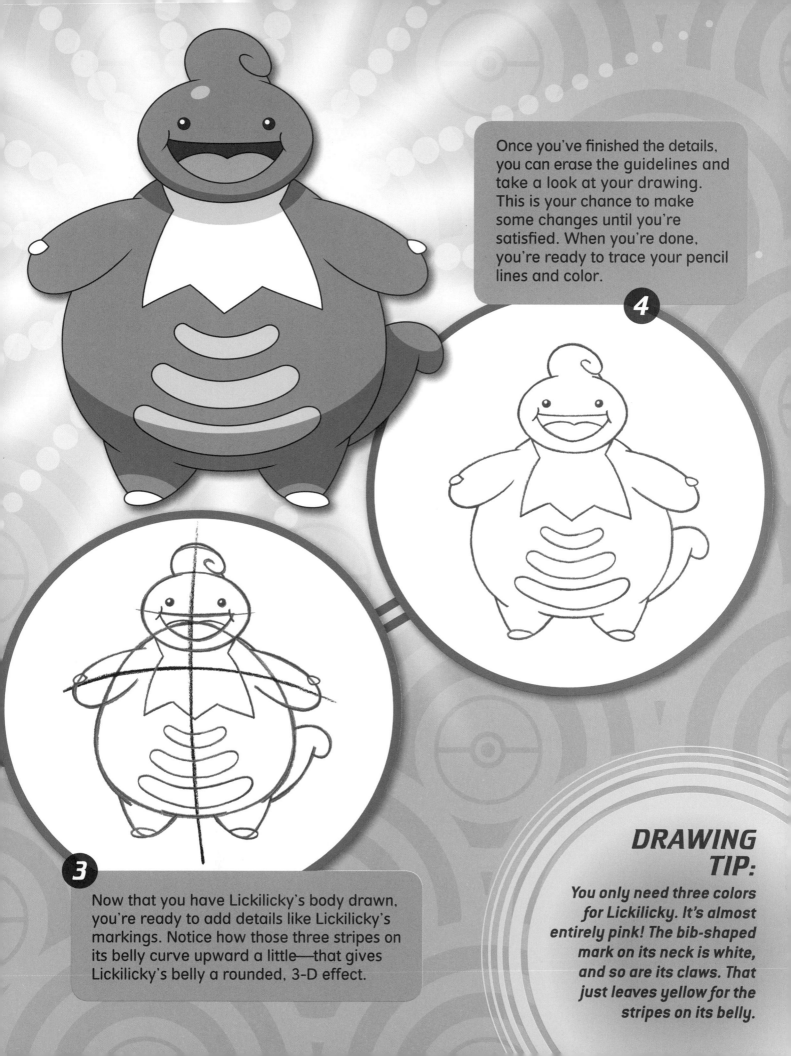

Once you've finished the details, you can erase the guidelines and take a look at your drawing. This is your chance to make some changes until you're satisfied. When you're done, you're ready to trace your pencil lines and color.

4

3

Now that you have Lickilicky's body drawn, you're ready to add details like Lickilicky's markings. Notice how those three stripes on its belly curve upward a little—that gives Lickilicky's belly a rounded, 3-D effect.

DRAWING TIP:

You only need three colors for Lickilicky. It's almost entirely pink! The bib-shaped mark on its neck is white, and so are its claws. That just leaves yellow for the stripes on its belly.

BUNEARY

Buneary are able to deliver powerful blows by uncoiling their ears. These hits are strong enough to destroy solid rock! Buneary also have impressive jumping abilities.

2 Use the guides to locate and sketch the eyes and mouth. Then add the ears and arms in the positions indicated. Note the short, straight vertical line that defines the attachment of the head to the body.

1 Start with just two action lines, then pencil in the three large ellipses (ovals) that will become the head, body, and foot. Note how the crisscross guides on the head oval strongly indicate the direction Buneary is facing. Use a half-oval shape to define the foot in the rear.

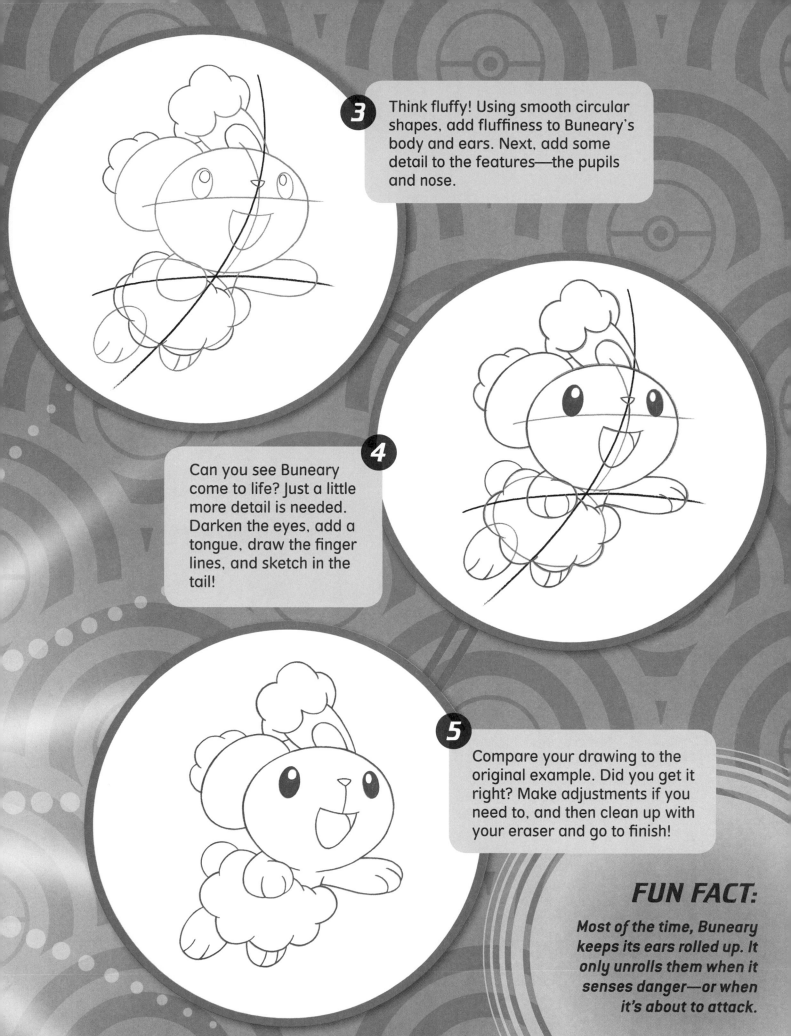

3 Think fluffy! Using smooth circular shapes, add fluffiness to Buneary's body and ears. Next, add some detail to the features—the pupils and nose.

4 Can you see Buneary come to life? Just a little more detail is needed. Darken the eyes, add a tongue, draw the finger lines, and sketch in the tail!

5 Compare your drawing to the original example. Did you get it right? Make adjustments if you need to, and then clean up with your eraser and go to finish!

FUN FACT:

Most of the time, Buneary keeps its ears rolled up. It only unrolls them when it senses danger—or when it's about to attack.

HAPPINY

Happiny always carries a round white stone that looks like an egg inside its pouch. If it likes you, it might offer the stone to you.

1 After sketching in the action lines, the real trick to drawing Happiny is the large oval shape that defines the entire structure of its body. So work carefully until you're sure you've got it right!

2 Widen your original oval at the bottom to allow for the pouch area and move on to sketch the features and hair. Note how the small floating oval in the last step is altered here to become a curlicue . . . every object has an underlying basic shape to structure it around.

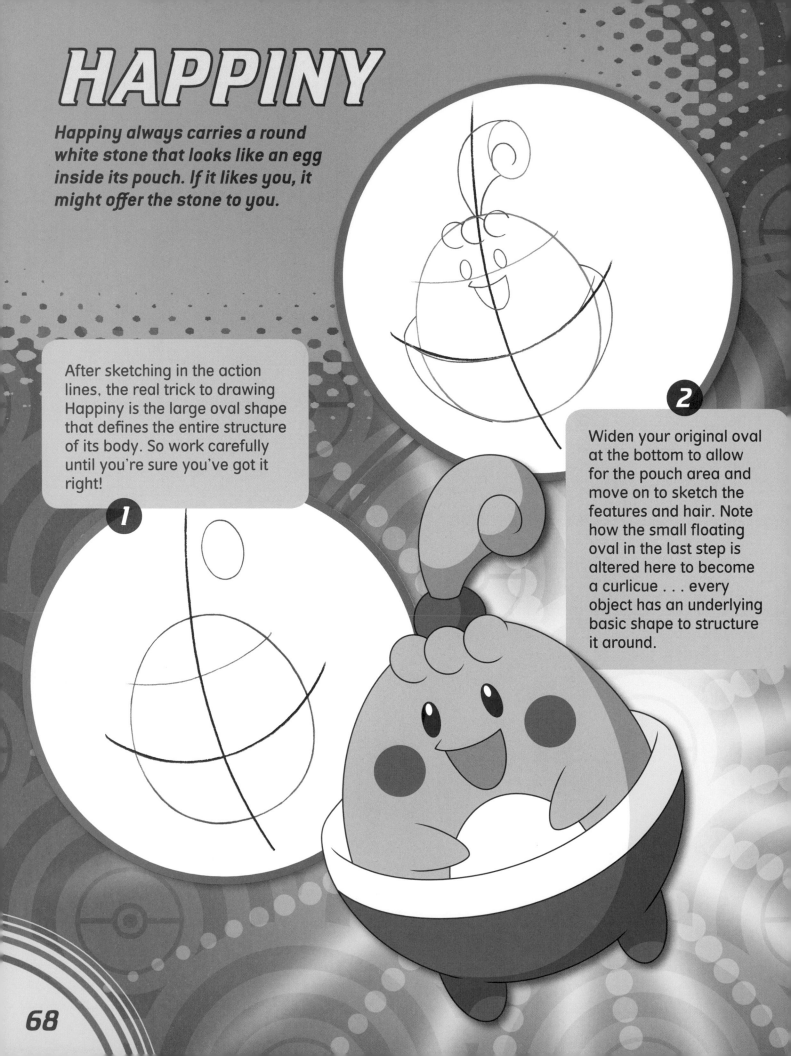

68

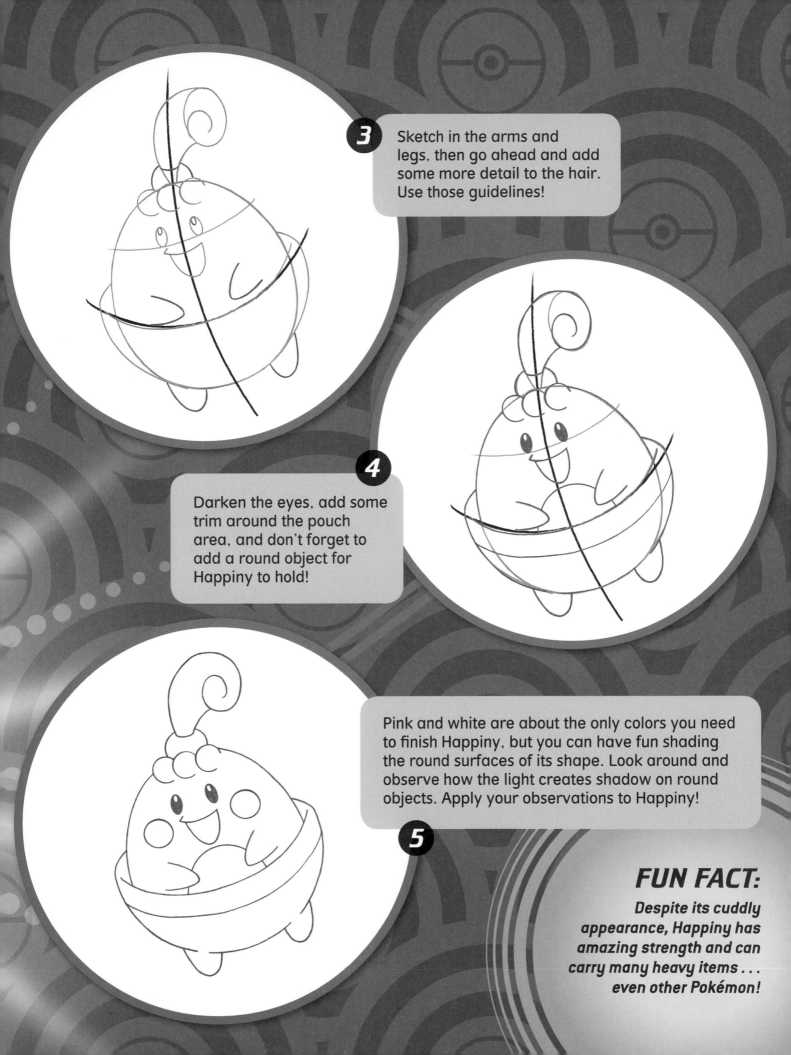

3 Sketch in the arms and legs, then go ahead and add some more detail to the hair. Use those guidelines!

4 Darken the eyes, add some trim around the pouch area, and don't forget to add a round object for Happiny to hold!

5 Pink and white are about the only colors you need to finish Happiny, but you can have fun shading the round surfaces of its shape. Look around and observe how the light creates shadow on round objects. Apply your observations to Happiny!

FUN FACT:

Despite its cuddly appearance, Happiny has amazing strength and can carry many heavy items . . . even other Pokémon!

PACHIRISU

Pachirisu show their affection for one another by rubbing their cheeks together. But they're sharing more than just friendly feelings—they're also sharing electric energy!

After the usual action lines, make a very large oval for the head and add the crisscross guides to it. Next, sketch the ovals for the feet. Where you place them along the vertical action line will determine how long the body will be, so be careful!

1

Locate and pencil in the eyes and mouth, then the ears. Overlap two small ovals for the front paws. Next, finish the body sides. The tail is just a single squiggle at this point.

2

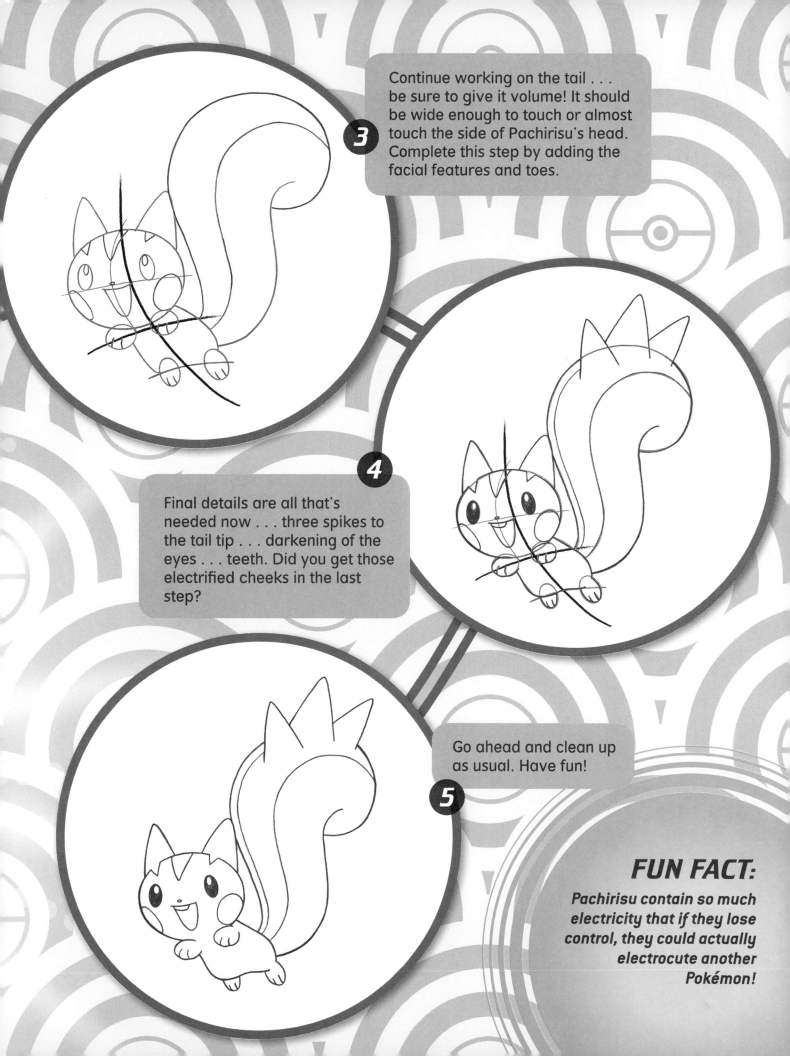

Continue working on the tail . . . be sure to give it volume! It should be wide enough to touch or almost touch the side of Pachirisu's head. Complete this step by adding the facial features and toes.

3

4

Final details are all that's needed now . . . three spikes to the tail tip . . . darkening of the eyes . . . teeth. Did you get those electrified cheeks in the last step?

Go ahead and clean up as usual. Have fun!

5

FUN FACT:

Pachirisu contain so much electricity that if they lose control, they could actually electrocute another Pokémon!

CROAGUNK

Croagunk inflates the poison sacs in its cheeks to create its trademark croak. The sound is so loud and startling, it often gives Croagunk a chance to slip in a poison attack against an opponent.

The features will be easier to place if you draw the oval for the cheek first and then sketch the mouth as a wavy line from the cheek to the other side of the circle. Note that the top and side of the head circle should be altered here to become the proper shape of Croagunk's head. Along the top horizontal action line, sketch the cylindrical shapes for the upper and lower arms, then add the feet.

Draw the single vertical action line and the two horizontal ones. Place a large circle for the head just off-center of the top axis. Then add an oval for the thigh on the lower horizontal action line. Now you have enough shapes in position to link the body shape. Sketch it in!

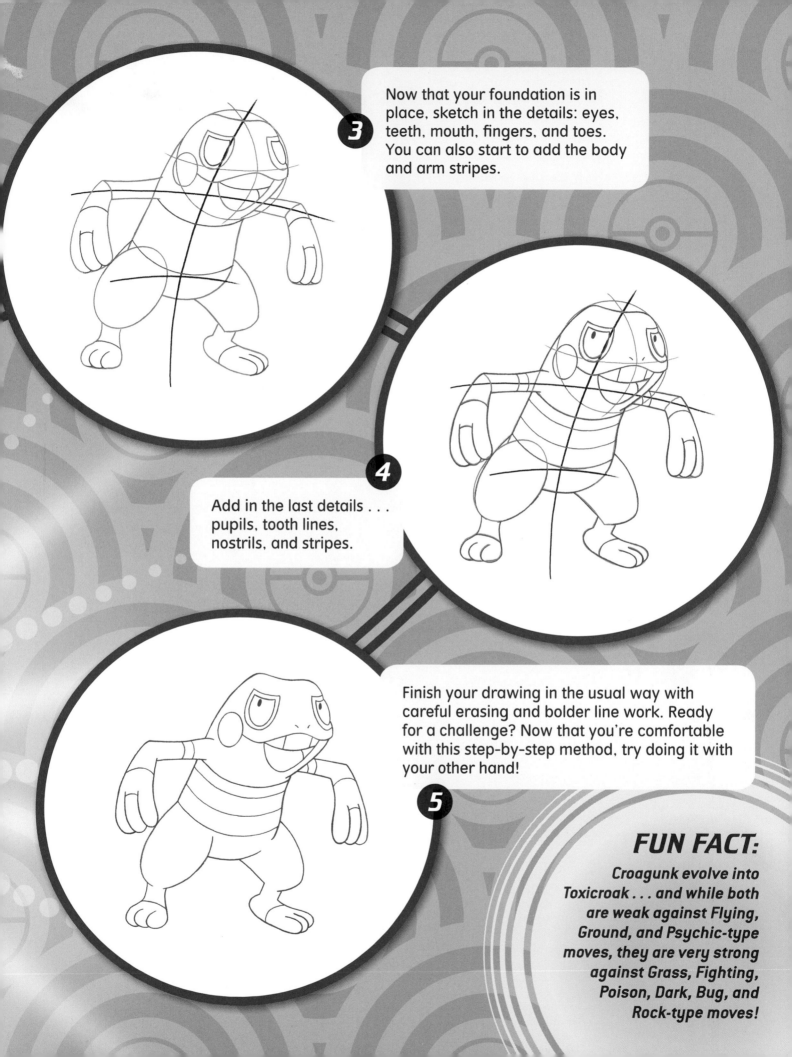

3 Now that your foundation is in place, sketch in the details: eyes, teeth, mouth, fingers, and toes. You can also start to add the body and arm stripes.

4 Add in the last details . . . pupils, tooth lines, nostrils, and stripes.

5 Finish your drawing in the usual way with careful erasing and bolder line work. Ready for a challenge? Now that you're comfortable with this step-by-step method, try doing it with your other hand!

FUN FACT:

Croagunk evolve into Toxicroak . . . and while both are weak against Flying, Ground, and Psychic-type moves, they are very strong against Grass, Fighting, Poison, Dark, Bug, and Rock-type moves!

AZELF

In Sinnoh, legends say that Azelf originated from the same egg as Uxie and Mesprit. Azelf is known to the people of Sinnoh as the Being of Willpower. You'll need some willpower and determination of your own to find out, because Azelf can be hard to find. It usually sleeps deep beneath a lake, but even while it sleeps, it helps to keep the world in balance!

1

This Azelf is flying gracefully through the air, so make your first guideline one big swoop. Use ovals for the shape of Azelf's head and body.

Now it's time to sketch in the lines of Azelf's body and tail. Make sure they flow together! Because Azelf is looking up, you'll want to draw its eyes closer to the top of its head.

2

Does your Azelf look like it's taking flight? Stick with your drawing and don't give up—sometimes, little changes make all the difference!

4

3

Now you can move on to the finishing details, like Azelf's eyes, mouth, and the decorations on its tail.

DRAWING TIP:

Azelf is light gray, with a blue face and curious, bright-yellow eyes. Don't forget to put in the highlights on its tail!

UXIE

Is this mysterious Pokémon sleeping? Not at all! Uxie's eyes are closed even when it's awake. Legend says that it brought the gift of intelligence to humankind. In Sinnoh, it is known as "The Being of Knowledge."

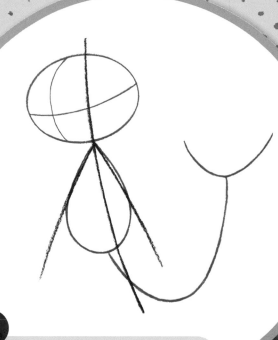

1 Put in your guidelines. As you add the oval for Uxie's head and a teardrop shape for its body, notice how Uxie's body and tail form the shape of a backward J.

When you draw Uxie's body, there are two points to remember. First, you can use a quick circle for the outer shape of Uxie's head. Second, don't forget to add that extra line to the lowest curve of Uxie's tail.

2

Hmm . . . is that a thoughtful Uxie you see when you erase your guidelines? Now's the time to adjust your details!

4

3

Just a few more details to go! Add Uxie's eyelids, mouth, and the lines on its head. You're not done with its tail yet—add some triangles and gem-like details.

DRAWING TIP:

Color Uxie's body a soft gray, and make its eyes and the top of its head yellow. You can make the red details shine like jewels if you add a little white highlight.

MESPRIT

The people of Sinnoh call Mesprit the Being of Emotion, and the stories say it was able to teach people about both sorrow and joy. Like Uxie and Azelf, Mesprit normally sleeps at the bottom of a lake. That doesn't mean it has to miss out on what happens on the surface, though— Mesprit can send its spirit soaring!

1

Start with your guidelines— but you knew that already, didn't you? Here, Mesprit's back and tail are aligned to form a nice straight line.

2

Add in features of Mesprit's head, feet, and tails. The outline of its eyes should be just above the guideline.

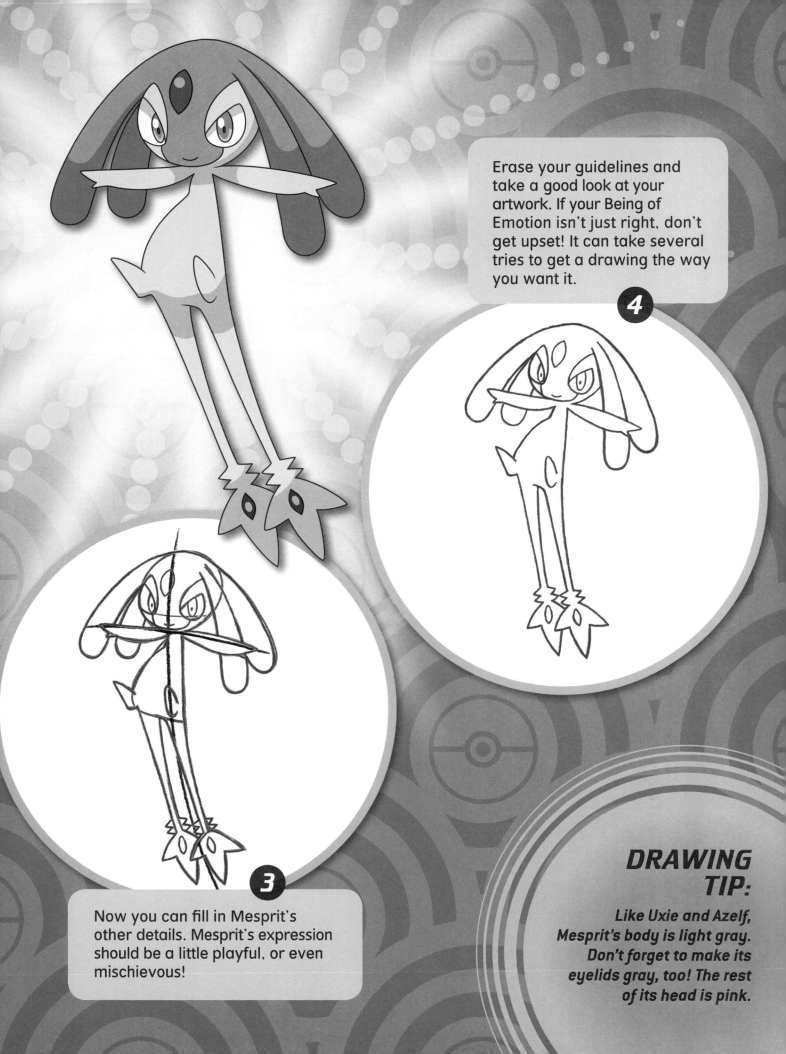

Erase your guidelines and take a good look at your artwork. If your Being of Emotion isn't just right, don't get upset! It can take several tries to get a drawing the way you want it.

4

3

Now you can fill in Mesprit's other details. Mesprit's expression should be a little playful, or even mischievous!

DRAWING TIP:

Like Uxie and Azelf, Mesprit's body is light gray. Don't forget to make its eyelids gray, too! The rest of its head is pink.

SNIVY

Snivy is one of the three Pokémon new Trainers in Unova receive from Professor Juniper. This clever Grass-type loves the sun—the more sunlight it soaks up, the swifter its movements in battle.

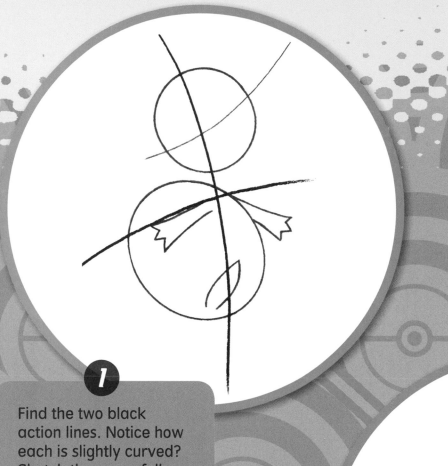

1

Find the two black action lines. Notice how each is slightly curved? Sketch them carefully onto your paper. Next, draw the large blue oval for Snivy's body and the smaller one for its head. Use the action lines to help line them up. Finally, add the arm shapes and the foot.

Look for the blue lines— these are the new shapes you'll add to your sketch. First, the large curved triangle; next, the eye and mouth. Use another oval to slim down the body and form the tail. Finish with the foot and shoulder.

2

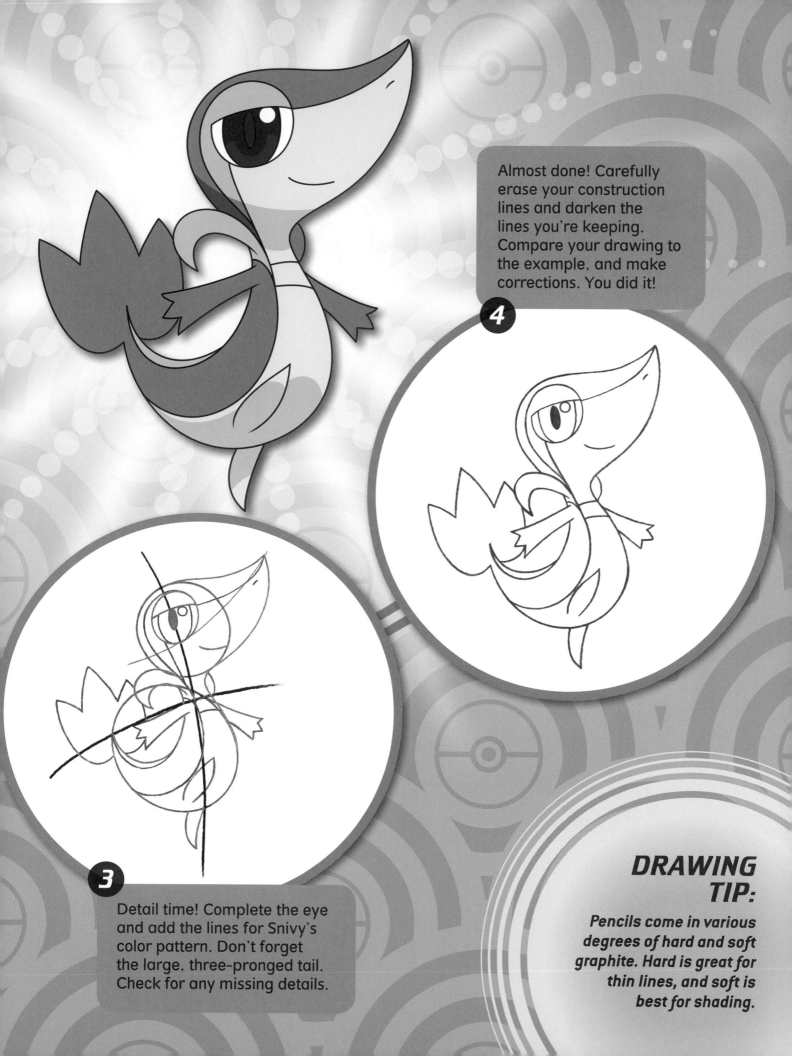

Almost done! Carefully erase your construction lines and darken the lines you're keeping. Compare your drawing to the example, and make corrections. You did it!

4

3

Detail time! Complete the eye and add the lines for Snivy's color pattern. Don't forget the large, three-pronged tail. Check for any missing details.

DRAWING TIP:

Pencils come in various degrees of hard and soft graphite. Hard is great for thin lines, and soft is best for shading.

TEPIG

Tepig is another one of the three Pokémon new Trainers in Unova receive from Professor Juniper. This little Fire-type can blow fire through its nose. If it catches a cold, the fire turns into plumes of black smoke.

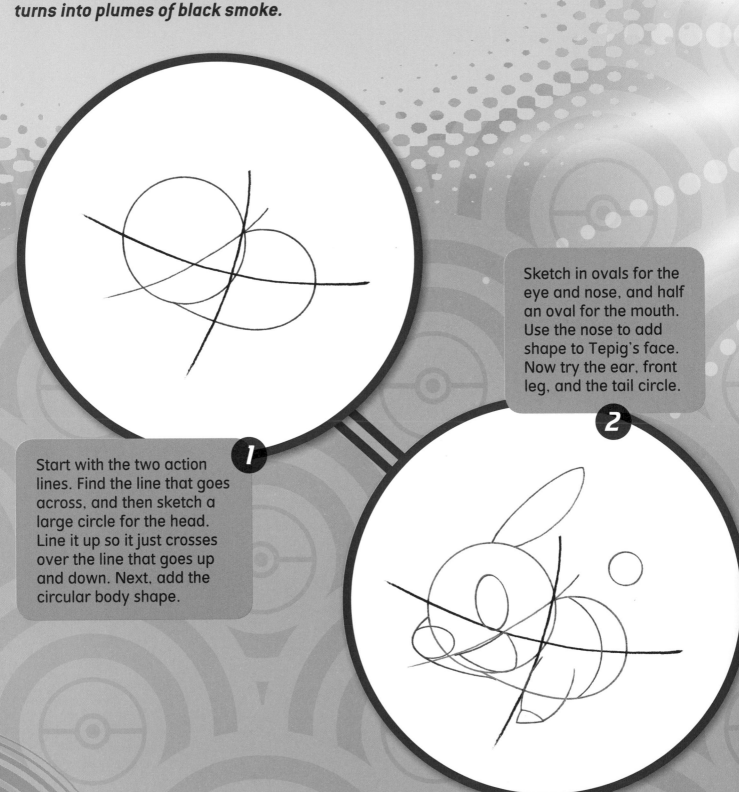

Sketch in ovals for the eye and nose, and half an oval for the mouth. Use the nose to add shape to Tepig's face. Now try the ear, front leg, and the tail circle.

1

Start with the two action lines. Find the line that goes across, and then sketch a large circle for the head. Line it up so it just crosses over the line that goes up and down. Next, add the circular body shape.

2

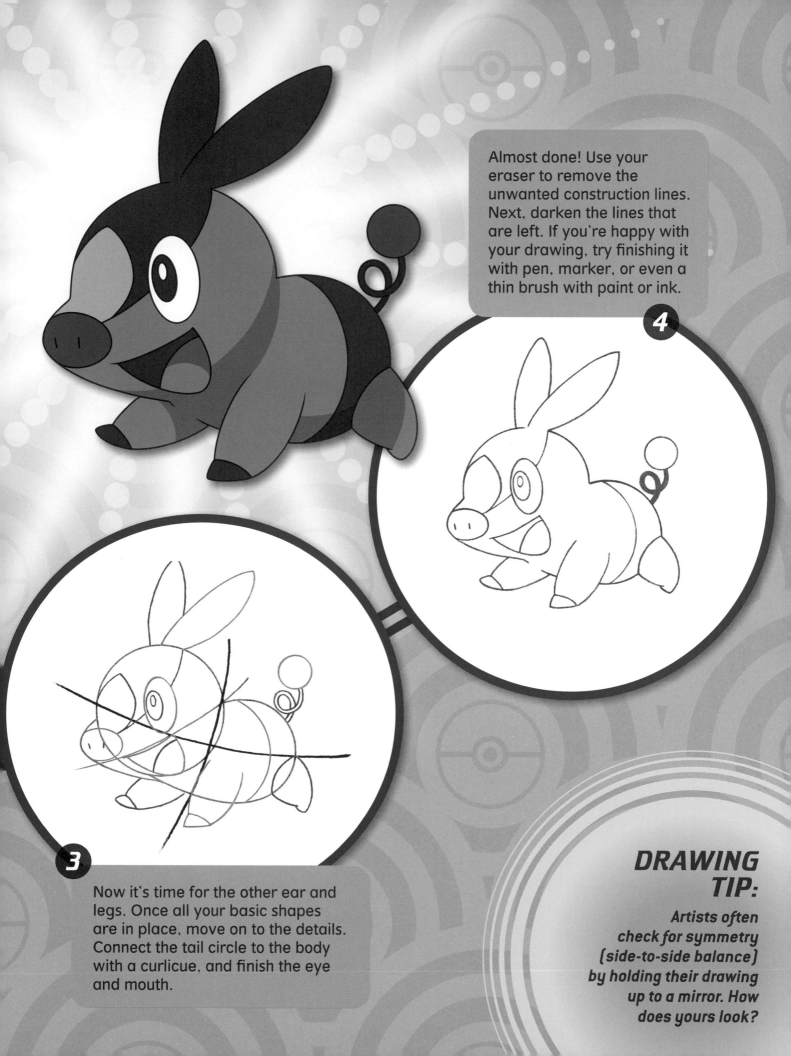

Almost done! Use your eraser to remove the unwanted construction lines. Next, darken the lines that are left. If you're happy with your drawing, try finishing it with pen, marker, or even a thin brush with paint or ink.

4

3

Now it's time for the other ear and legs. Once all your basic shapes are in place, move on to the details. Connect the tail circle to the body with a curlicue, and finish the eye and mouth.

DRAWING TIP:

Artists often check for symmetry (side-to-side balance) by holding their drawing up to a mirror. How does yours look?

OSHAWOTT

Oshawott is the third of the three Pokémon Professor Juniper gives to new Trainers in Unova. A Water-type also known as the Sea Otter Pokémon, it is very strong against Fire-types. The scalchop on its stomach can be detached and used as a blade during battle.

1 Draw the action lines lightly, and place the large head circle just above the place where the lines meet. Then sketch smaller crosshairs on the head to help you place Oshawott's features. Add a smaller circle just below the head.

2 Using the small crosshairs as guides, sketch the eyes, nose, and mouth. Pencil in the arm and leg shapes, and then draw the semicircle in the center of Oshawott's stomach.

Grab your eraser, clean up your drawing, and finish it with bolder lines. Oshawatt is ready for battle!

4

3

Begin adding your final details, including Oshawott's freckles, toes, ears, and the frills around the collar. Finish the scalchop on the stomach. Don't forget Oshawott's tail!

DRAWING TIP:

You can shade your drawings with the side of your pencil. Or try dipping your finger into the shavings from your pencil sharpener and using your finger as a crayon!

ALOMOMOLA

Alomomola are covered in a special healing substance. They have been known to assist injured Pokémon they find in the sea and bring them safely to shore.

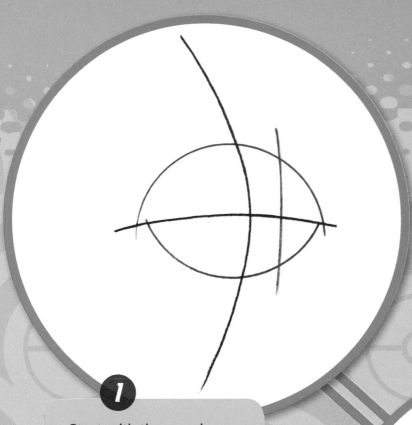

1

Start with the usual crossed action lines. Then place the two large semicircles. Add another line to the right of where the action lines cross. You'll use this to place Alomomola's features.

Following the curve of the action lines, draw the top fin, and then the bottom. It's okay to turn your paper to make it easier. Shorten the body at the end. Next, draw the side fin, eye, and mouth.

2

Compare your drawing to the original. If it looks good, erase your sketch lines and strengthen the lines you need to keep. Don't forget to add color!

4

3

Concentrate on the details now. Pencil in elements of the eye; shorten the nose; add lines to the fins . . . you're almost there!

DRAWING TIP:

Many artists like to use layers of tracing paper for each step of their sketches. It saves time erasing later, plus there's less chance of smudging.

AXEW

Axew often marks trees with its strong, sharp tusks. If a tusk breaks, a new one quickly grows in to replace it. This fierce Dragon-type also uses its tusks to crush the berries it eats.

1

Draw the action lines and place the large oval for the head. Then add the crosshairs; you'll use them later to draw the features. Put another oval below the first—this will become Axew's body.

2

Draw the large triangular fin on the back of the head, and then form the eye shape, mouth, and tusks. Finish with the arms and legs.

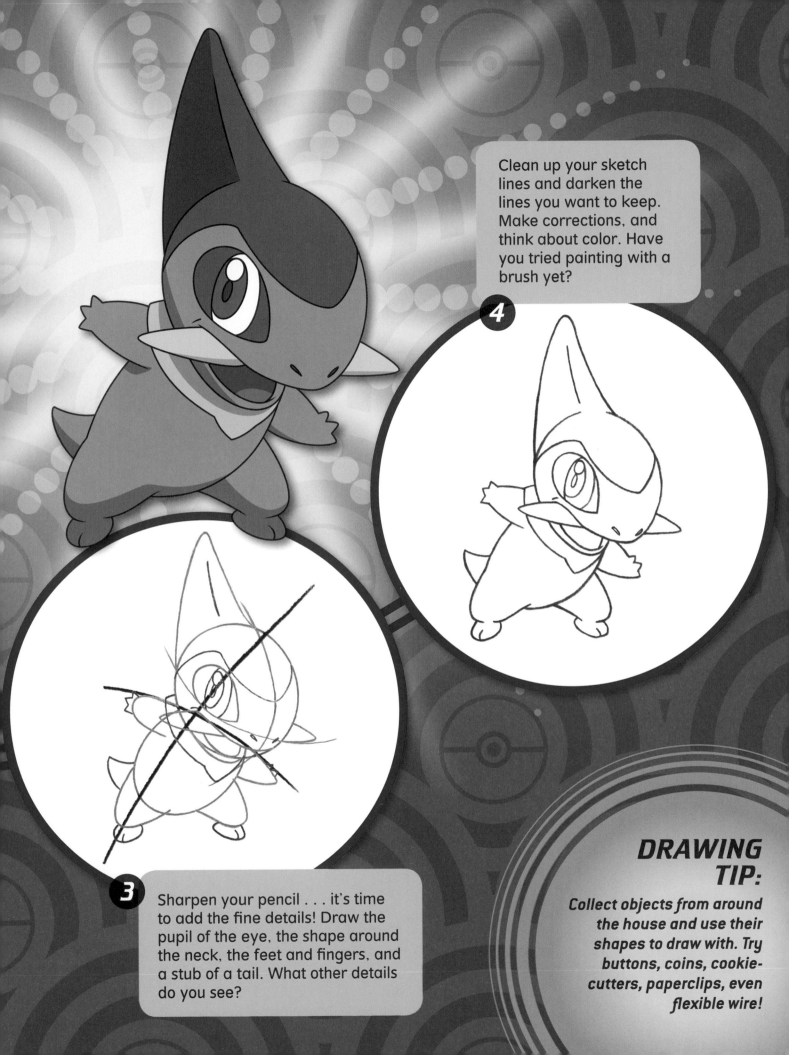

Clean up your sketch lines and darken the lines you want to keep. Make corrections, and think about color. Have you tried painting with a brush yet?

4

3 Sharpen your pencil . . . it's time to add the fine details! Draw the pupil of the eye, the shape around the neck, the feet and fingers, and a stub of a tail. What other details do you see?

DRAWING TIP:

Collect objects from around the house and use their shapes to draw with. Try buttons, coins, cookie-cutters, paperclips, even flexible wire!

MUNNA

Munna eats the dreams of both people and Pokémon. When it eats a good dream, it lets out a pink-colored mist. People whose dreams are consumed by Munna forget what they dreamed about.

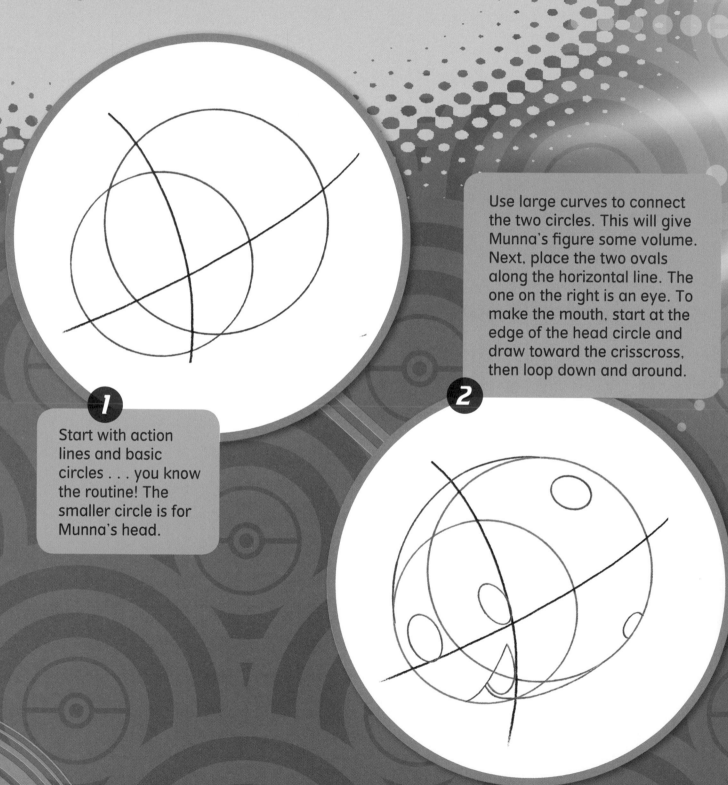

1 Start with action lines and basic circles . . . you know the routine! The smaller circle is for Munna's head.

2 Use large curves to connect the two circles. This will give Munna's figure some volume. Next, place the two ovals along the horizontal line. The one on the right is an eye. To make the mouth, start at the edge of the head circle and draw toward the crisscross, then loop down and around.

Erase your unwanted sketch lines, and then darken the lines you want to keep. Do you see how all the things you want to draw can be broken down into simple shapes?

4

3

Add the short triangle shapes that form Munna's feet. Next, add the eyelashes and the patterns on its back.

DRAWING TIP:

Take one of your drawings, turn it over, and blacken the back of the paper with the side of your pencil. Place it over a clean sheet and trace the drawing. Instant copy!

SANDILE

Sandile moves along below the sand's surface, with only its nose and eyes aboveground. A dark membrane shields its eyes from the sun, and the warm sands prevent its body temperature from dropping.

1
Sketch your two action lines, then place the head circle. Use a thinner oval to define Sandile's eye. Shape the body, then look for the circle of Sandile's belly and draw the wavy line to form its lower body and tail.

2
Start with the oval that will become the tip of Sandile's nose. Then move on to the snout, mouth, and second eye oval. Use a large half oval to form the eye socket. Look at the leg shapes carefully, and then copy them onto your sketch.

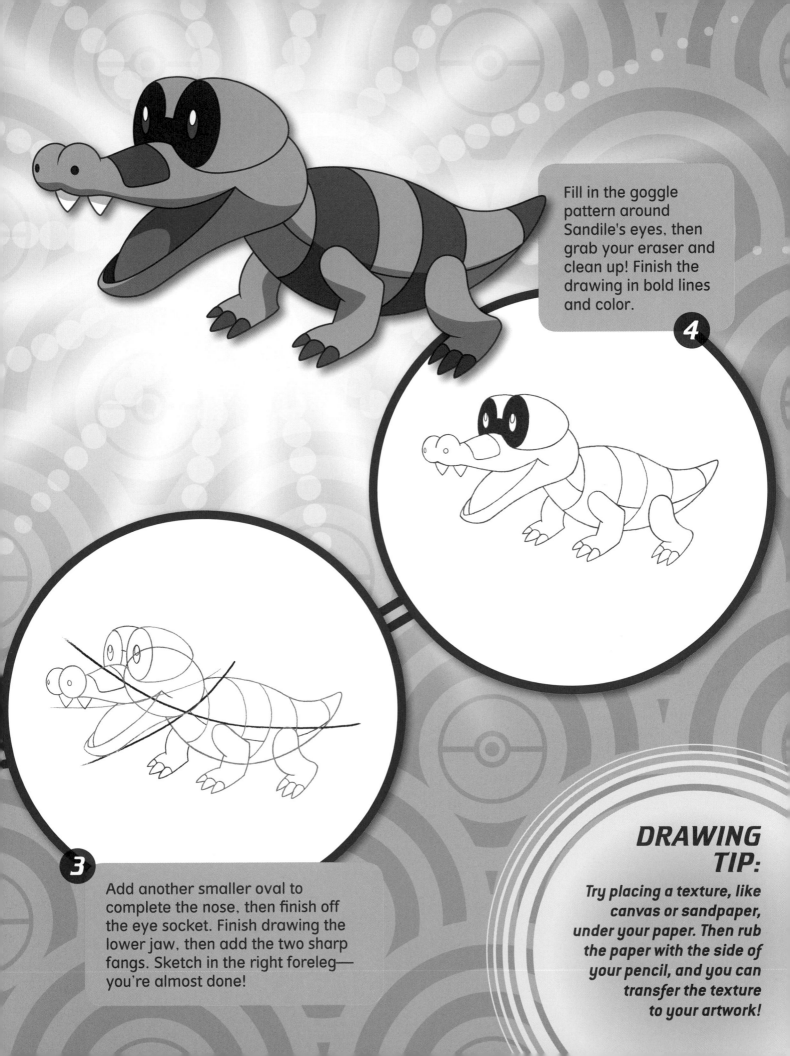

Fill in the goggle pattern around Sandile's eyes, then grab your eraser and clean up! Finish the drawing in bold lines and color.

4

3

Add another smaller oval to complete the nose, then finish off the eye socket. Finish drawing the lower jaw, then add the two sharp fangs. Sketch in the right foreleg—you're almost done!

DRAWING TIP:

Try placing a texture, like canvas or sandpaper, under your paper. Then rub the paper with the side of your pencil, and you can transfer the texture to your artwork!

DEERLING

Deerling changes color with the turning of the seasons. Its Spring Form is bright pink; its Summer Form is green; its Autumn Form is orange; and its Winter Form is brown.

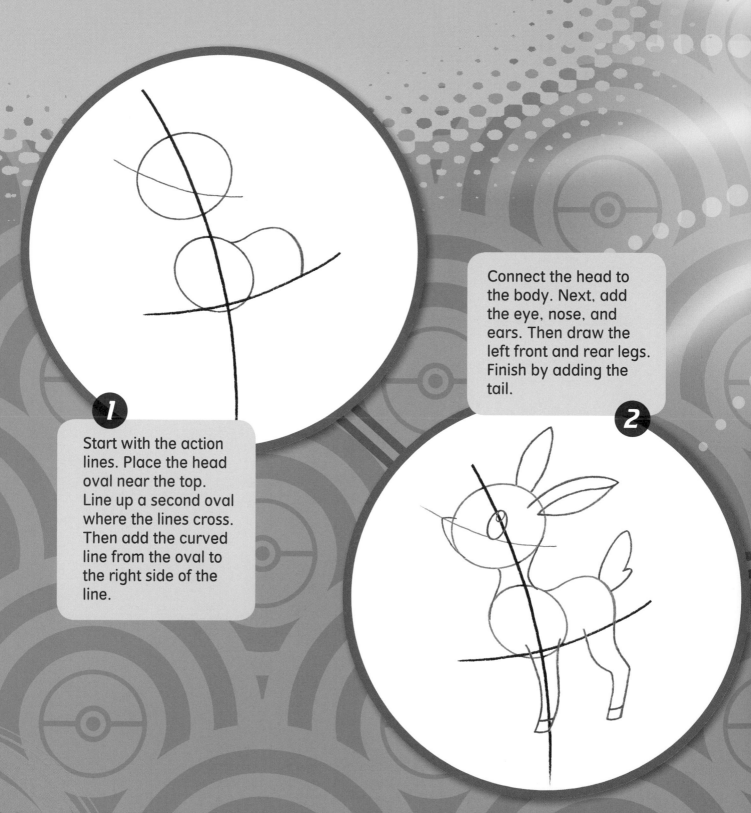

1 Start with the action lines. Place the head oval near the top. Line up a second oval where the lines cross. Then add the curved line from the oval to the right side of the line.

2 Connect the head to the body. Next, add the eye, nose, and ears. Then draw the left front and rear legs. Finish by adding the tail.

Clean up your drawing and start coloring! You've got four different color choices: pink, green, orange, and brown. Why not try them all?

4

3 Copy the legs you drew in the last step to form Deerling's front and rear legs. Now sketch in the flower on top of the head, and finish the eye and nose. Don't forget Deerling's color pattern.

DRAWING TIP:

People once used white correction pens for things written on typewriters. Now they're a great tool for artists—for corrections, or just for drawing in white!

PIDOVE

Pidove doesn't mind a crowd. It lives in the city and often gathers in flocks in big public areas, like parks and plazas.

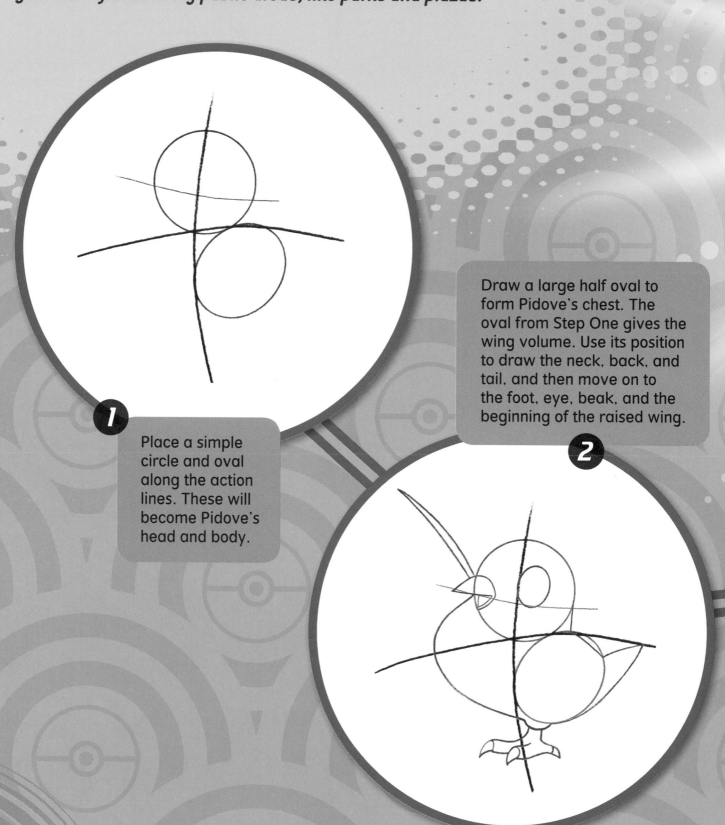

1 Place a simple circle and oval along the action lines. These will become Pidove's head and body.

2 Draw a large half oval to form Pidove's chest. The oval from Step One gives the wing volume. Use its position to draw the neck, back, and tail, and then move on to the foot, eye, beak, and the beginning of the raised wing.

Do your usual cleanup, and you've got another Pokémon ready to add to your drawing Pokédex!

4

3

Start by drawing the loops that form the raised wing. Next, add the crest to the head and the other foot. Now it's detail time! Complete the eye, nose, and wing bands.

DRAWING TIP:

A small fishing tackle box makes a great art kit! The little slots for hooks and lures are perfect for erasers and pencil sharpeners.

MINCCINO

Minccino are tidy creatures that love to clean and groom. They greet others of their kind by brushing their tails together. They also use their tails as brooms.

1

Sketch the action lines and place the head shape—it's almost a perfect circle. Put the crosshairs on the head, and then draw a square with rounded corners for Minccino's body.

2

It's time for Minccino's huge ears. Check your sizing; the ears should be larger than its head! Draw the eyes and mouth, and then add the arms and legs.

Do your usual cleanup . . . erase some lines, darken others. Now might be a good time to try a coloring technique you haven't used before. Watercolors, anyone?

4

3

Bring on the details: the tufts of fur on Minccino's head and chest, and its paws and toes. Finish with the long, sweeping tail.

DRAWING TIP:

TV and movie animators often sketch in light blue and then darken their work with black. The color contrast makes it easier to see mistakes and correct them.

WOOBAT

Woobat lives in dark forests and caves. It sleeps in caves, hanging from its nose, which uses suction to stick to cave walls. It leaves a heart-shaped mark behind.

1 It may look complex, but Woobat is actually pretty simple. Draw the action lines, make a very large circle, and add two simple wing shapes.

2 Complete the wings, and then add the nose shape with a heart inside. The mouth has one triangular tooth.

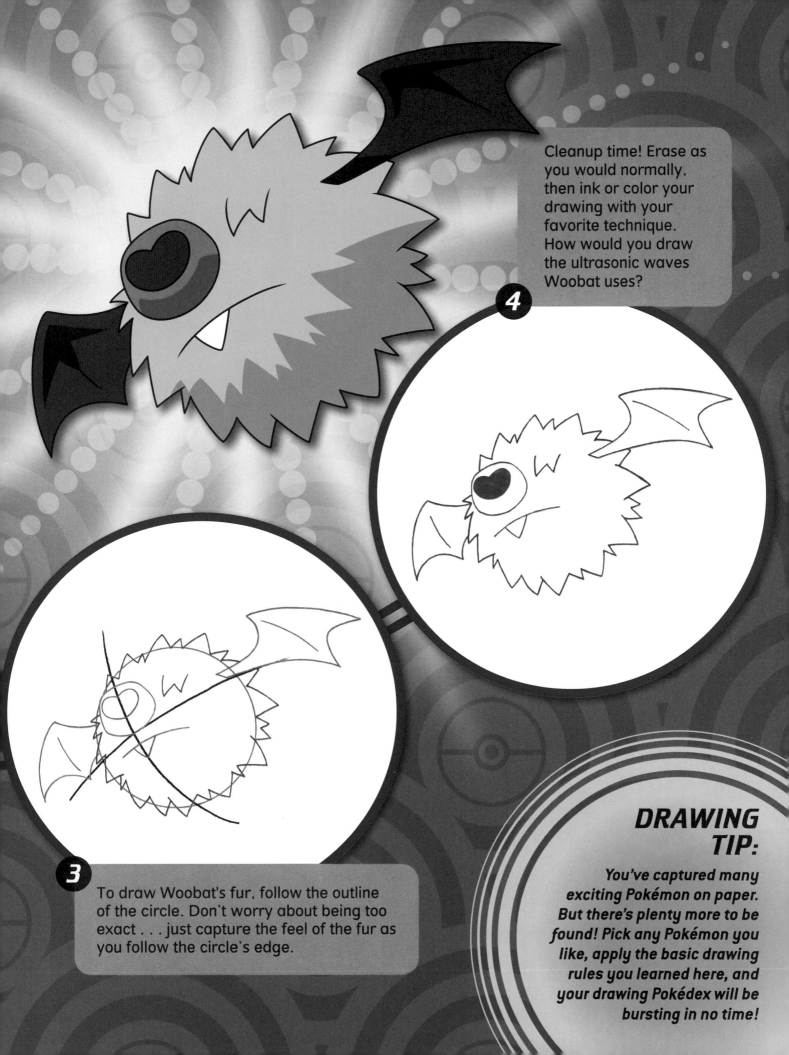

Cleanup time! Erase as you would normally, then ink or color your drawing with your favorite technique. How would you draw the ultrasonic waves Woobat uses?

4

3

To draw Woobat's fur, follow the outline of the circle. Don't worry about being too exact . . . just capture the feel of the fur as you follow the circle's edge.

DRAWING TIP:

You've captured many exciting Pokémon on paper. But there's plenty more to be found! Pick any Pokémon you like, apply the basic drawing rules you learned here, and your drawing Pokédex will be bursting in no time!

CHESPIN

Look out, opponents! When Chespin flexes its soft quills, they become tough spikes with sharp, piercing points. It relies on its nutlike shell for protection in battle, so use a bright green to make it pop!

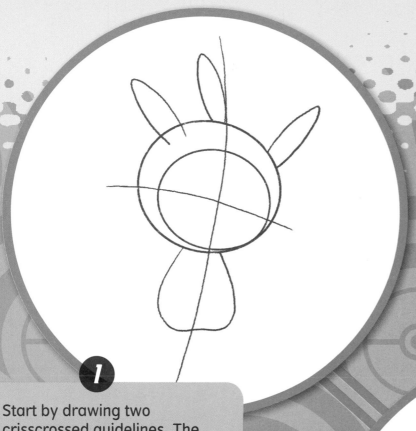

1

Start by drawing two crisscrossed guidelines. The spot where they meet will be the center of the face. Draw a circle inside a circle to start. Then draw the basic shapes of the body and quills.

Draw long ovals for Chespin's feet, arms, tail, and the soft quills on top of its head. Now use the guidelines to help you draw the face. See how the nose is on the right side of the vertical guideline? The mouth sits just below the horizontal guideline.

2

3

Start adding details like Chespin's tongue, tooth, and toes. Then stand back and take a good look at your drawing. Are any details missing?

4

Time for the fun part! Erase any lines you don't need. Then add color. Chespin's quills are a bright grass green, and the tip of its tail is a dazzling red. When the color is done, you can trace over the outlines with a thin black marker.

FROAKIE

In this pose, Froakie is super-alert to any changes in its environment. The foamy white bubbles that cover its turquoise body protect this Water-type Pokémon's sensitive skin from damage. When you're ready to color in Froakie's bubbles, try letting the white of the paper show through.

1 Start by drawing the shape of a football. Then add two upside-down Us on top for the eyes. Finish up with a rectangular body. Now stop and do a quick check. Are all the shapes where you want them to be?

2 Draw an oval inside each eye. For the nose, turn your paper sideways and draw the number 8. Froakie's arms start where the head and body meet. Trace the arms on scrap paper a few times before adding them to your drawing.

3 Inside the left edge of each eye, draw an oval inside an oval. Does Froakie look watchful? Now, take your time and draw the back legs. Using half circles and curves, draw the foamy bubbles that protect Froakie's sensitive skin.

4 Stand back and check your drawing. Which lines need to be erased? Which lines need to be darker? Does Froakie have three fingers on its hands, but only two on its back legs? Did you remember to add the dark blue stripe between the eyes? Great! Now finish off your drawing with color!

FENNEKIN

The warm, orangy-red details in this Fire-type's ears, eyes, and tail warn opponents that Fennekin means business. Fennekin likes to charge up before a match by snacking on twigs. You might want to grab a healthy snack to get energized for drawing!

Fennekin's pointy nose sits on the horizontal guideline. Draw an oval for the eye where the two guidelines meet. Then sketch in some curved lines where you want to draw the second ear. Next, add a fat teardrop for the tail. Practice the legs on scrap paper before adding them to your drawing.

2

Lightly sketch in guidelines. Use them to figure out where to draw the oval for Fennekin's head and the jellybean shape for its body. Then add a curvy triangle for the ear.

1

Erase the lines you don't need. Now step back and take a good look at your drawing. Are the ears as big as the body? How about the legs? Make any tiny fixes, and you're ready to color!

4

3 Take your time drawing the details on Fennekin's body. Those ears and tail are important! Fennekin uses its plush tail for blazing moves like Tail Whip and Fire Spin, and its ears blast intense heat to keep opponents far away.

DRAWING TIP:

Don't be afraid to trace! It's not cheating, and it will help you learn size and proportion . . . all artists do it from time to time!

SWIRLIX

Swirlix's love of sweet snacks makes its fur as sticky as cotton candy. Here's a tip: To keep your hand from sticking to your drawing, keep a piece of scrap paper between you and the paper.

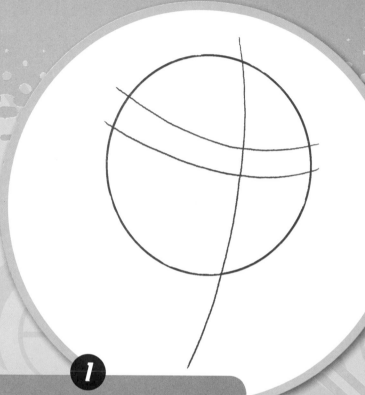

1

Start by drawing a big circle. Then draw one vertical guideline and two curved horizontal guidelines. The top line shows where the eyes and nose will go. The bottom line is for the mouth.

Add the basic shapes of the face, legs, tail, and the puffs on top of Swirlix's head. Use your guidelines to help you. Now stop and take a look. Are all the features where you want them to be?

3

Ready to focus on details? Add a small oval inside each eye and a tongue sticking out of the mouth. Draw curves around the outline of Swirlix's body to make it look puffy, like a cotton ball. Then draw a tail at the bottom.

4

Erase extra lines and smudges. When you color Swirlix, try using the white of the paper for the body and light lavender for the shadows. Does your Swirlix look like it's ready to spring off the page?

LITLEO

When a young Litleo is ready to grow stronger, it spends time on its own developing moves like Flamethrower and Noble Roar. Don't worry about making mistakes as your drawing grows stronger. Learning to draw Pokémon takes time and lots of practice.

1

Start your drawing of Litleo with lots of circles. What's the secret to drawing round circles? Sometimes, the faster you draw them, the rounder they turn out. Go ahead and practice on scrap paper first.

Draw more circles for the back paw, tail, eyes, and ears. Then connect the front paws to the body with straight lines. Use the guidelines to help you position the nose and mouth between the eyes. Is your drawing already starting to look like Litleo?

2

Erase extra lines and get ready to color! During a battle, Litleo's mane gives off intense heat. That's why it's red while the rest of the body is shades of brown!

4

3

This step is all about details. Pick a starting point like the paw pads and make sure you draw them all. Connect the back leg to the body with two short curved lines. Don't forget the tuft of hair on top of Litleo's head.

DRAWING TIP:

Everything around you is made of basic shapes. Put some tracing paper over a favorite photo or magazine picture and draw as many basic shapes as you can find!

PANCHAM

For a small Pokémon, Pancham has big moves like Body Slam, Crunch, and Karate Chop. You have big decisions to make before you start to draw. Will your drawing of Pancham take up the whole paper? Or will it leap off the page?

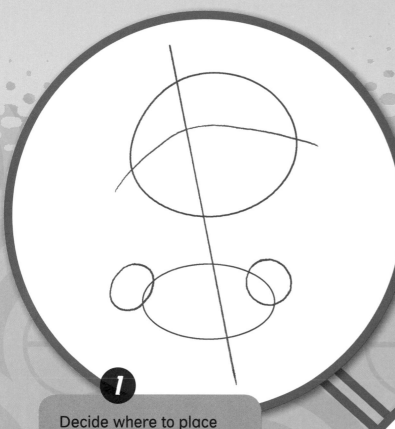

1 Decide where to place Pancham on the paper. Then lightly sketch in guidelines and some basic shapes. The vertical guideline is slanted to give a sense of motion.

Use the guidelines to help you position the shapes in the face. Then connect the head to the body with a big, upside-down U. Next, draw the arms on an angle. The right arm looks shorter than the left because it's farther away.

2

3

Clean up the outline of Pancham's body. Then start at the top and add details like a zigzag of hair, ovals inside the eyes, and another zigzag for the teeth. Don't forget to draw a leafy sprig next to the mouth. This leaf helps Pancham track its opponents' movements.

4

Do you need to make any changes to your drawing? Does Pancham look like it's leaping into the air? If not, maybe its bottom paws are not high enough. When you're ready, get out your colors. Here's a tip: Use a darker color for the inside of the mouth than for the tongue.

TYRUNT

This Rock-and-Dragon-type Pokémon has powerful jaws that could crush a car! It also has mighty moves like Earthquake, Dragon Claw, and Stomp. Tyrunt lived millions of years ago, but your drawing will be brand-new. Practice the hard parts on scrap paper before you start.

1

Step One is all about the big decisions. Will your drawing of Tyrunt take up the whole page or just a small part? Draw the guidelines closer together this time. Then sketch in the basic shapes. Tyrunt is leaning forward, so the head and body fall on the same horizontal line.

The oval you drew in Step One shows where Tyrunt's massive leg connects to its body. Draw a small arm right in front of the oval. Then add a tail and a zigzag around its neck. Now focus on the jaw. It juts out from the circle you drew for the head.

2

Erase extra lines and smudges. Now double-check your drawing. Does anything need fixing up? Is the head almost the same size as the body? Did you draw claws on the hands and feet? Good job! You did it!

4

3 Draw in the back leg. Then take some time to add details. If they look confusing, pick a place to begin, such as the tail. Then add other details bit by bit—like the half rectangles on the back leg, the fang, and the horns on its head.

GOOMY

This Dragon-type Pokémon is covered with a slippery membrane that makes its opponent's punches and kicks slide right off it. Goomy protects this membrane from the sun by taking shelter in damp, dark places. Remember to keep your drawing of Goomy away from the sun, too! Bright colors fade in direct sunlight.

1

Start by drawing a big circle. Then attach a few curved lines that look like a cape. Keep your lines light at first— that way, they'll be easy to erase or draw over.

Draw two small dark ovals for eyes, one on each side of the vertical guideline. Then add two long upside-down U shapes to the top of Goomy's head. Next, replace the bottom line of its body with a wavy line.

2

116

Erase any lines you don't need. Now quick! Color in Goomy's lavender-and-purple body and bright green cheeks before it evolves into Sliggoo!

4

3 Draw two ovals for cheeks between the two horizontal guidelines. Connect them with another wavy line. Then add two smaller upside-down U shapes to the head.

DEDENNE

Dedenne's whiskers are a very important part of this drawing. Dedenne uses them like antennae to send long-distance messages via electrical waves. It also uses them to store up electrical energy for powerful moves like Thunder Wave and Volt Switch.

1 Start with two curved guidelines. Then draw the basic shapes for Dedenne's body. The ovals for the head and body should overlap.

2 Dedenne can soak up electricity through its tail, so make sure the tail is longer than its body. Add circles for the cheeks and ovals for the eyes. Then draw a short angled line on top of each eye to make Dedenne look ready for action.

3
Now that the basic outline of the body is in place, it's time to add details. Draw the antennae-like whiskers. Then add fingers, toes, a tongue, and a star shape at the tip of the tail.

4
Almost done! Erase the starter shapes. Then break out the colors! Color in the lightest parts of Dedenne's body first. If you use markers or paint, wait until the lightest brown is 100% dry before you paint the darker browns and red on top. That way, your colors won't run into each other!

119

BUNNELBY

Bunnelby's ears are as long as its entire body! Bunnelby uses them like shovels to dig big holes in the ground and for moves like Double Slap and Mud-Slap. The ears are so strong, they can even dig through thick tree roots!

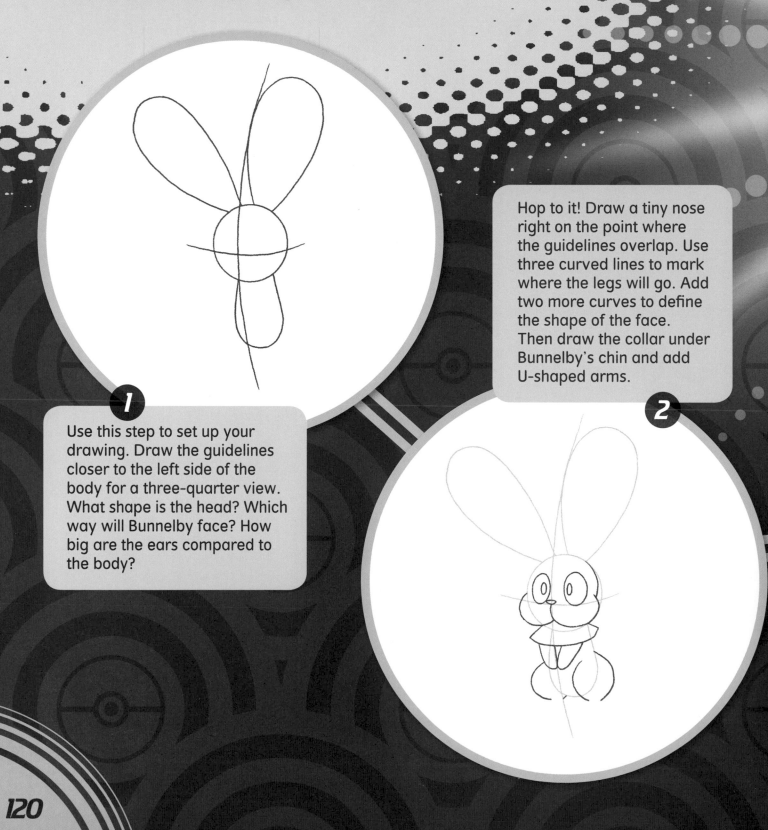

1

Use this step to set up your drawing. Draw the guidelines closer to the left side of the body for a three-quarter view. What shape is the head? Which way will Bunnelby face? How big are the ears compared to the body?

2

Hop to it! Draw a tiny nose right on the point where the guidelines overlap. Use three curved lines to mark where the legs will go. Add two more curves to define the shape of the face. Then draw the collar under Bunnelby's chin and add U-shaped arms.

4

Call in the cleanup crew! Erase any extra lines, smudges, or mistakes. Then color in this Normal-type Pokémon with shades of brown and gray before it bounces off the page!

3

There are lots of details in this step, so take your time. Draw whiskers, spots, and two front teeth. Don't forget the tail, fingers, and teardrop shapes inside the ears.

ROWLET

This night flyer gathers energy from the sun all day so it can play all night. You may want to energize yourself with a healthy snack before drawing this Alolan first partner Pokémon!

1

Start by drawing a big circle for the head. Then draw two crisscross guidelines that divide the circle into four parts. The top two sections should be smaller than the bottom sections.

Draw an oval for Rowlet's beak at the top of the vertical guideline. Then add two more ovals for the eyes. Now turn your paper sideways and draw the number eight around the eyes and beak.

2

Now hang up your drawing and take a step back. Are the eyes smaller than the beak? Do the feet look ready to unleash a flurry of attacks? Then color in your Rowlet and go!

4

3

Are you ready for details? Sketch in two W-shaped lines for the feet and two U-shaped lines for the wings. Then add a small oval inside each eye. Finish up with a curved line for the smile!

DRAWING TIP:

Now that you can draw Rowlet, try drawing it using Leafage to blast Team Rocket with sharp green leaves!

LITTEN

Trainers often have a hard time getting this solitary Pokémon to trust them. Do you trust your drawing skills? Try using a circle guide, oval guide, and a ruler to give this finicky Fire Cat Pokémon a more polished look.

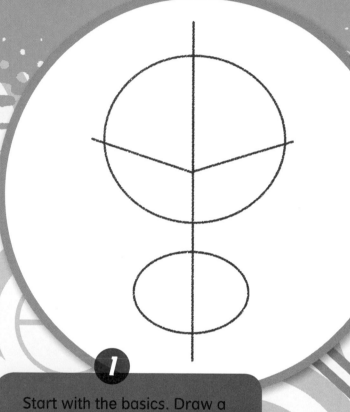

1

Start with the basics. Draw a vertical guideline. Then sketch a big circle for the head and a smaller oval for the body. Make sure the two shapes don't touch or overlap. Inside the bigger circle, draw two angled lines for Litten's brow.

Before you begin this step, practice the shapes by tracing them on scrap paper. Then draw two U shapes under the guidelines for eyes. Add the mouth, ears, and whiskers. The legs are basically two vertical lines with a curve at the bottom.

2

3

Pick a starting point and begin adding details little by little. The design on Litten's forehead is symmetrical. That means it's the same on one side of the guideline as it is on the other. And don't forget the tail!

4

Step back, do a cat stretch, and take a good look at your drawing. Are any details missing? Scratch in a few more and get ready to color. This fiery kitty has bold coloring, including a black body, red design, and bright yellow eyes.

POPPLIO

This Water-type Pokémon is super talented—and hardworking! Popplio practices making water balloons with its nose every day! Sometimes the balloons are big and strong. Sometimes they pop. When you make a mistake in a drawing, don't sweat it! Think about what you can do differently next time. Then try, try, try again!

1

Start by sketching a big, uneven X. Use a ruler if you like. The longer guideline will run straight through Popplio's left flipper. Then draw the basic shape of the body. You'll be using lots of curved lines in this drawing!

Trace the shapes of the flippers and nose on scrap paper a few times to get used to them. Then use light, loose lines to add them to your drawing. The nose sits where the two guidelines crisscross.

2

Do a drawing check! Popplio's left flipper should be bigger than the right flipper because it is closer to you. Does your drawing need other tweaks?

4

3

Add details like a U-shaped ear and Popplio's curvy collar. Does the eye look complicated? Break it down! Draw one small white oval inside a bigger, darker oval. What about the mouth? It's a U shape with a curved line inside for the tongue.

DRAWING TIP:

Now that you're a pro, draw Popplio blowing a water balloon big enough to sail across the sea!

PYUKUMUKU

When Pyukumuku get scared, they spew out their innards to strike their opponents. But you don't have to be afraid of this drawing. Practice drawing the starfish on Pyukumuku's face by tracing the shape over and over again on scrap paper.

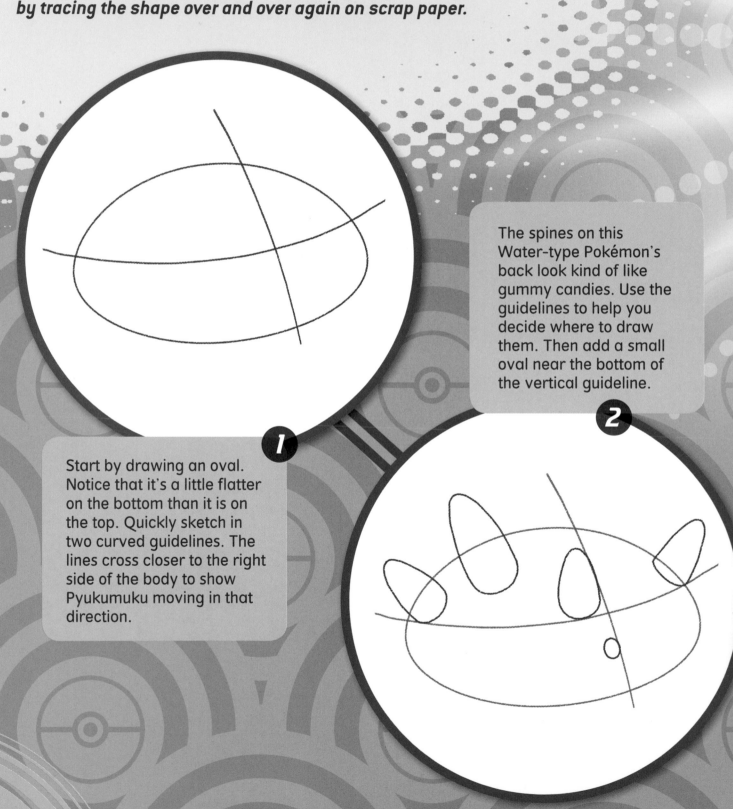

The spines on this Water-type Pokémon's back look kind of like gummy candies. Use the guidelines to help you decide where to draw them. Then add a small oval near the bottom of the vertical guideline.

2

Start by drawing an oval. Notice that it's a little flatter on the bottom than it is on the top. Quickly sketch in two curved guidelines. The lines cross closer to the right side of the body to show Pyukumuku moving in that direction.

1

Erase those guidelines and get ready to color. If you're using markers, fill in the fuchsia of the spines and let them dry before you color in the body. This will keep your colors from bleeding into one another.

4

3

Remember that starfish shape you practiced before starting this piece? Go ahead and draw in the lower right-hand section of the body now. Then add a cottontail on the other end.

DRAWING TIP:

Now that you can draw Pyukumuku, can you draw a whole school of them among the coral at the bottom of the sea?

KOMALA

This dreamy Pokémon is always cuddling a log or its Trainer's arm. But it's no slouch. And neither are you! This drawing may be challenging. Try tracing the final step on scrap paper as practice before you begin. And remember to break each step down into smaller steps as you go along. You've got this!

1 Start with a quick oval. Then draw two curved guidelines to show that Komala is facing left. Now add three fast, sketchy lines to block out a space for the body and log. Remember to stay loose. This stage is not about perfection!

2 Block in the rest of the basic shapes, like an oval for the nose and floppy curved lines for the ears. The arms and legs are also simple curved lines. Then do a quick check. Is everything where you want it to be?

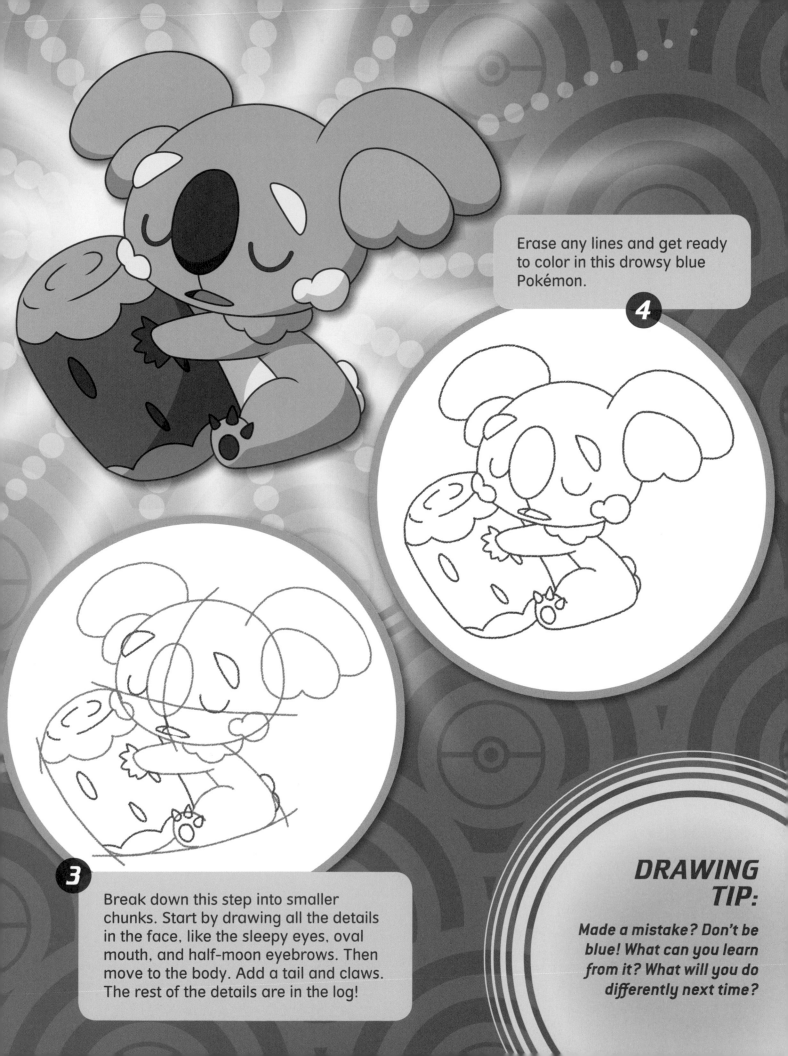

Erase any lines and get ready to color in this drowsy blue Pokémon.

4

3

Break down this step into smaller chunks. Start by drawing all the details in the face, like the sleepy eyes, oval mouth, and half-moon eyebrows. Then move to the body. Add a tail and claws. The rest of the details are in the log!

DRAWING TIP:

Made a mistake? Don't be blue! What can you learn from it? What will you do differently next time?

ROCKRUFF

This friendly Rock-type Pokémon is a great companion for a journey through the Alola region. Make this drawing of Rockruff friendlier by using the vertical guideline to create symmetry. The right side of Rockruff is a mirror image of the left side. If you fold your paper in half, the outlines should match up!

1

When breaking a drawing down into basic shapes, squint your eyes so you don't see too many details at once. If you squint at this picture of Rockruff, you'll see a circle sitting on top of a rectangle.

Take your time when placing features like the eyes, ears, and legs. And keep your lines light in case you need to erase them. Notice that the ears flop over the top of the head.

2

3 Too many details? Break it down! The guidelines you drew in Step One divide your drawing into four sections. Draw the details in one section at a time. Don't forget to show the back legs peeking out from behind the front legs.

4 Erase the original guidelines and the outlines of the starting shapes. Then compare your drawing to the one in the book. Is anything missing? If not, it's time to rock out with color! This pup has bright blue eyes and a pink nose.

TOGEDEMARU

Togedemaru has long, spiny fur that bristles during storms to attract lightning. Warm up your drawing arm by sketching lightning-fast circles on scrap paper. Sometimes, the faster you draw a circle, the less you worry, and the rounder it turns out!

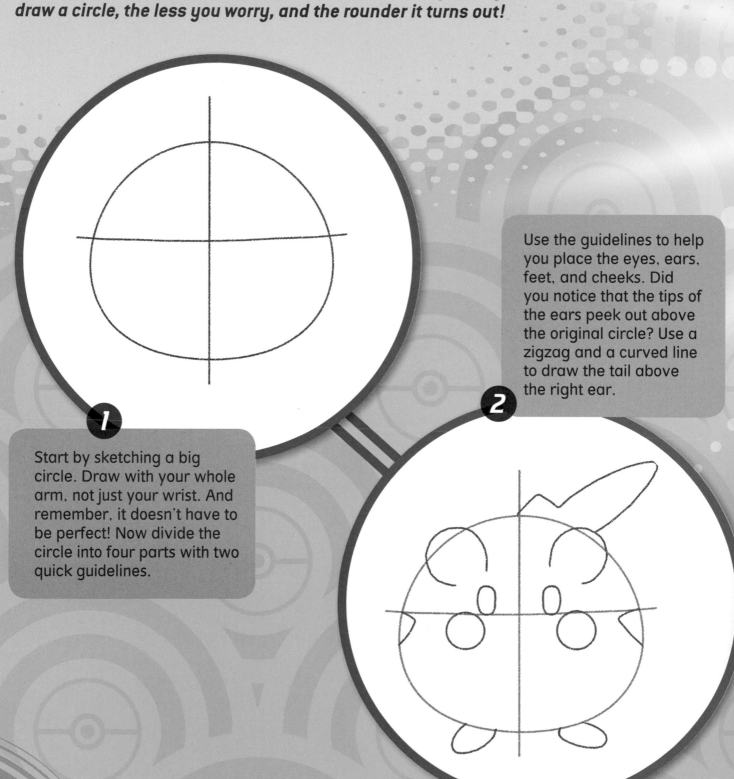

1

Start by sketching a big circle. Draw with your whole arm, not just your wrist. And remember, it doesn't have to be perfect! Now divide the circle into four parts with two quick guidelines.

Use the guidelines to help you place the eyes, ears, feet, and cheeks. Did you notice that the tips of the ears peek out above the original circle? Use a zigzag and a curved line to draw the tail above the right ear.

2

4

You got this! Erase the original guideline and any other lines you don't need. Would you like to change or adjust anything? If not, it's time to color! Togedemaru's cheeks are yellow, but most of its body is gray and white.

3

Do you like where you've placed all the features? Great! Then add details like the eyes, nose, and mouth. And use V-shaped lines around the edges of the circle to show off Togedemaru's spiky fur.

BEWEAR

This super-strong Pokémon has big arms that are great for giving bone-crushing bear hugs. And this drawing of Bewear is made of big shapes, so loosen up your drawing arm by drawing jelly beans, circles, and rectangles on a big piece of scrap paper. Remember to move your whole arm as you draw, not just your wrist!

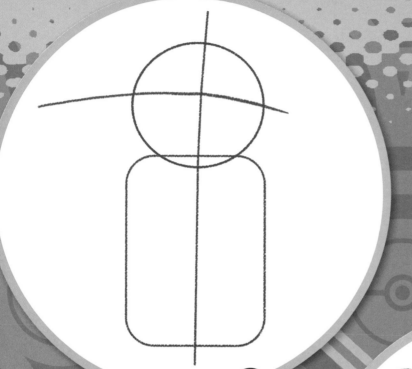

1

Start by drawing a circle on top of a rectangle with rounded corners. Make sure they overlap a tiny bit. Then quickly sketch in two crisscrossed guidelines. The horizontal guideline should be curved to help you draw Bewear's face in the next step.

Use the guidelines to place Bewear's eyes and football-shaped snout. Draw two ears outside the top half of the circle. Then use big, sweeping movements to sketch in the arms and legs.

2

Add color, like a bubblegum pink head and paw pads. When you're finished, you can trace over the outlines with a thin black marker.

4

3

Most of the details in the paws and face are circles and ovals. Take some extra time to sketch the curved lines that make up Bewear's tail. They'll help your drawing begin to look 3-D.

DRAWING TIP:

Try drawing this Bewear catching Team Rocket or sending them off with a new blast!

MIMIKYU

How many different kinds of lines can you find in this drawing of the Disguise Pokémon? Squiggly lines, wiggly lines, straight lines, zigzags, and curves are all hiding inside this finished drawing . . . just like the real Mimikyu hides under a rag so it doesn't scare away new friends!

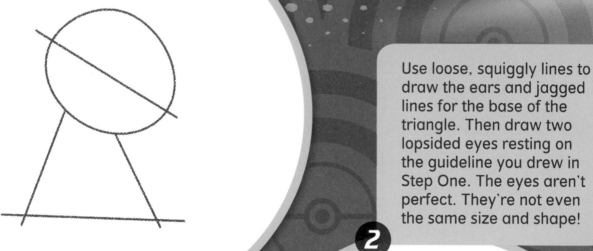

1 Start by drawing a triangle. Then draw an oval leaning off the top of it. Sketch a tilted horizontal line through the middle of the oval. Don't worry about getting them exactly right.

2 Use loose, squiggly lines to draw the ears and jagged lines for the base of the triangle. Then draw two lopsided eyes resting on the guideline you drew in Step One. The eyes aren't perfect. They're not even the same size and shape!

4

Almost done! This stage is about refining. Erase any lines you don't need and tweak the outline of the head and body. Now that you can draw this Ghost-and-Fairy-type, can you sketch Team Rocket's Mimikyu hurling a Shadow Ball at Pikachu?

3

Add detail lines to the ears and body and sketch in the tail. Then draw two ovals for cheeks. Connect them with a thick zigzag for the mouth. Here's a tip: Draw the Mimikyu's facial features with a crayon for the line quality!

BOUNSWEET

Mallow's Bounsweet loves to race Ash's Pikachu across the sand. But you don't have to race to finish this drawing. Take your time and practice any challenging shapes on scrap paper before adding them to your final piece.

Connect the leaves with a smaller oval. Then draw two tiny ovals for the eyes. Using curved lines, sketch in the basic cloud shape at the bottom of Bounsweet's body. Now draw a V shape below the circle for the tail.

Start with a big circle for the body. Then add two smaller ovals to the top for leaves. Now sketch in a quick, curved guideline. Make sure it's a little off-center for a three-quarter view.

3

Time to add details—like a sweet smile! Draw a curvy stem at the top of the head. Then sketch details on the leaves and body. Now do a check. Are all the lines where you want them to be? Suh-WEET!

4

Erase any smudges and extra lines. Ready for a color explosion? Bounsweet's leafy cap is bright green, and most of its body is a rich berry or fuchsia. Let the white of the paper show through for the frilly band at the bottom.

LUCARIO

Lucario has strange powers. When it evolves, it learns to sense auras—and to control them. This Fighting-and-Steel-type Pokémon is a formidable opponent. It's also a challenging drawing, so take your time and go for it! You're a Pokémon drawing expert!

Build Lucario's body around the stick figure. The back leg is smaller than the front leg because it's farther away. Now draw the eyes, ears, and snout.

1

Start with a stick figure. It helps to figure out early on where you want to put the arms and legs.

2

Look back and forth between Steps Three and Four. Did you miss any details or forget to erase any lines? Do it now!

4

3

This step is all about details—in the paws, the ears, and on the face. Practice drawing spikes on scrap paper before you add them to your drawing.

DRAWING TIP:

Do you want your drawing to look 3-D? Imagine shining a bright light on Lucario. What parts would the light hit? These areas are the highlights. The parts that wouldn't get light fall into shadow.

CONGRATULATIONS!
YOU'RE A POKEMON DRAWING CHAMPION!

Now that you know how to draw so many powerful Pokémon, what kinds of adventure will you draw next? What stories will you tell?

Litten evolving into Torracat?
Rowlet evolving into Dartrix?
Popplio evolving into Brionne?

Use your imagination—what happens next is up to you!